OCCULT GEOMETRY

INTERPRETS AND EXPLAINS SYMBOLS, NATURE'S UNIVERSAL LANGUAGE. SHOWS HOW GOD GEOMETRIZES TO PRODUCE THE UNIVERSE AND MAN AND THAT IN UNDERSTANDING HIMSELF, MAN UNDERSTANDS THE BIG UNIVERSE

By
DR. A. S. RALEIGH

A COURSE OF PRIVATE LESSONS GIVEN
TO HIS PERSONAL PUPILS

THE HERMETIC PUBLISHING COMPANY
3006 LAKE PARK AVE.   CHICAGO, ILL., U. S. A.

Copyright, 1932 by
The HERMETIC PUBLISHING COMPANY
Copyrighted and Registered at Stationers' Hall,
London, England
(All Rights Reserved)

CONTENTS

	LESSON I	Page
The Circle		7
	LESSON II	
The Line		12
	LESSON III	
The Triangle		17
	LESSON IV	
The Cross		23
	LESSON V	
The Swastika		29
	LESSON VI	
The Diamond		35
	LESSON VII	
The Pentagram		44
	LESSON VIII	
The Hexagram		51
	LESSON IX	
The Seven-Pointed Star		57
	LESSON X	
The Cube		64
	LESSON XI	
The Sphere		70
	LESSON XII	
Squaring the Circle		76

LESSON I

THE CIRCLE

The CIRCLE has from the earliest antiquity been employed as the symbol for Eternity and Unity. The CIRCLE is a line beginning at a point and traveling in a curve until it returns to the same point, consequently, it has no beginning and no end.

It is for this reason employed as the symbol of Eternity,— Eternity being in the strict sense of the word, beginningless and endless. Everlasting is not eternal for the reason that a thing may have a beginning although having no end, but that which is eternal is without beginning and without end. For this reason the circle, which is geometrically the same as Eternity in time, is employed as the symbol of Eternity.

Again, the Circle is employed to symbolize the Universe for the Universe is without beginning and without end in space, there being no point where it begins and none where it ends, that is to say, there is nothing outside of the Universe, it includes all things within its own compass and therefore, it is symbolized by the Circle.

Again, the Circle is used to symbolize Fate or Necessity,— as there is no beginning and no end and as the Circle of Necessity revolves, sooner or later, the Point comes. Further, it symbolizes repetition in history, all things repeating themselves from time to time, as the revolving returns to the same point.

It also symbolizes the cyclical law, for as the wheel turns the cycle returns again. Thus a new cycle begins, the cycle here being symbolized by each turn of the wheel, and so all through Nature we find this continual repetition of the cyclical law.

OCCULT GEOMETRY

The Circle is also used as a symbol of Unity, representing the one which contains all things within itself. Differentiation is caused by the energy going in two directions, but as long as Unity is preserved, the circular form must remain.

It will be quite possible to realize the reason for using the Circle as the symbol of Unity when we understand that it is formed by reason of the circling of forces round its center of gravity, the center of gravity here being an imaginary point in the middle of the Circle equally distant from each part of the Circle. In this sense the Circle is the form which energy assumes as it circles around its center of gravity. In other words, it is the figure of the whirl, and as all things in the Universe originate in a whirl, in the whirl which goes to form the Universe, it will, therefore, be seen that the Circle symbolizing the whirl, must perfectly represent the first creative impulse. It thus becomes the symbol of Creation, but each whirl expressing a given fiat, which is in turn the expression of an idea. The Circle is the expression in form of that idea. It is the Circle which the idea takes, giving the circular motion of substance under the influence of the energy imparted by the idea. It, therefore, represents Creation by the idea, likewise the Creation of a single form by a single idea,—in other words, specific as opposed to general creation.

It must not be assumed that the Circle has simply been employed in an arbitrary manner as the symbol of Creation and Unity; on the contrary, the creative idea cannot possibly express itself in any other form than that of the Circle. The whirl being the first motion growing out of the idea, the fiat continues to whirl the substance under the energizing impulse of that idea, therefore, Creation must always be through the whirl. As energy operates upon substance through the whirl, it must at all times describe a Circle. As long as that Circle is maintained, no variation of the creative impulse is possible, hence simple creation must be the result. In order for differentiation of manifestation to take place, it is necessary that the motion should be altered from the Circle to some variation corresponding to the new form. Therefore, the Circle symbolizes Creation and Unity, it being the circular character of the motion which maintains

THE CIRCLE

the integrity of the creation, this guaranteeing the undifferentiated expression. As this circular motion is maintained the tendency is to draw the energy acted upon this motion to that point where the velocity is the greatest. In other words, there is one direction of force represented by a whirling point. All substance responding in the slightest degree to this whirling point is at right angles to the same, but by reason of the whirl, is drawn after it, thus forming converging lines, resulting in so many currents of force flowing in the direction of, or gravitating to the whirling point, the result being a stream ever flowing toward the center, and at the same time, moving in the direction of the central stream. This stream of energized substance is, therefore, crowding on that point of greatest energy, at the same time being guided in its whirl by that force. The result is, the center around which the energy is whirling becomes deserted, the substance all flowing outward from the center of force, the attraction of the center of force being sufficient to maintain the center of substance, resulting in the formation of a ring. Thus the Kosmic activity must express itself in a series of rings. It is utterly impossible for any homogeneous motion to manifest anything through form. For this reason the Circle has been employed as the symbol for the homogeneous, and as the substance will continue to whirl in this form until differentiation takes place, it will logically follow that the continuity of the first whirl must always perpetuate the circular form. The Circle consequently symbolizes the symbol of Unity and that of Continuity, the two ideas, Unity and Continuity being the foundation of Eternity. Likewise, as there is no point in a Circle stronger than another, as the energy is active at all points alike, we have no beginning, no energizing point, but the entire Circle is gradually energizing itself. Thus, we have an idea of Eternity, as something inter-active as well as self-active.

The Circle has been used to symbolize Creation because Creation is through circular motion; to symbolize Eternity because Eternity is a Circle having no beginning and to symbolize Unity because the Circle is a unit of motion, as the expression of unity of ideas.

OCCULT GEOMETRY

Likewise, the Circle has been used as the symbol of God, of Deity, and why? Because Deity is self-derived, is not dependent upon another, but has its center of gravity within itself, the beginning point of the Divine being in himself, not in another. His motion is around a vacuum, that is, he does not revolve around anything else, but only around that which is not. God is his own center of gravity. For this reason He is symbolized by the Circle. Divine Energy must always flow in a circular form, likewise, all manifestations of Divinity as so many circles revolving around the Divine Center, at the same time revolving within the Divine circumference. Divinity is consequently described as a Circle whose center is everywhere and whose circumference is nowhere.

The Circle again represents the Universe as the Macrocosm, likewise each manifestation as the Microcosm. Again, every manifestation of the manifestation becomes circular. Thus we see the circular motion ever the manifestation of the homogeneous.

One form of the Circle is a serpent with its tail in its mouth. The serpent is not a natural circle, but is ordinarily a line and having beginning and end, thus representing the Law of Opposites, but when he swallows his tail the two opposites are brought together, are swallowed up by each other, or more usually one of the opposites is swallowed by the other. Thus in the conjunction of opposites, we have balance, which again expresses itself in the Circle. Life everlasting is thus secured through the merging of the two homogeneous activities. In other words, the heterogeneous is swallowed up in the homogeneous, thus bringing differentiation back into Unity. The end is swallowed up in the beginning, thus beginninglessness and endlessness are made possible, but there is this difference between the two circles; the true circle is an ever expanding manifesting Circle, while the Serpent Circle becomes a contracting circle. It is the return to Unity; it is differentiation swallowing itself, this reuniting is Unity. The true Circle symbolizes evolution, the Serpent Circle involution and in some instances devolution. It is the retrograde motion, which returns back, —the throw-back, in other words. It is for this reason that

THE CIRCLE

the Serpent swallowing its tail has ever been associated with the idea of Unity among those philosophers and religionists, who originated the Divine Unity and undertook by their own power to bring Unity out of diversity, this being the usurpation of the Divine prerogative by man; consequently it must result in the expression of the destructive principle of nature. The Serpent Circle is, therefore, ever the symbol of the destructive, inversive Magi, while the true Circle is the symbol of the expansive, eternal, creative unity, coming forth from the Divine Center. However, it does not symbolize manifestation in the sense of differentiation, but rather the direct creation of one thing from a single idea.

LESSON II

THE LINE

The LINE represents motion in two opposite directions. It is, consequently, the geometrical presentation of the Law of Opposites, the Circle representing Unity, because motion in one direction. One motion will always move in a circle, but when two opposite motions are introduced, we have the Line.

We should realize that when a Circle begins to move outward at the antipodes, it will gradually put forth two points which will, in time draw out into a line. Thus, the Line is motion moving from the center outward in two directions, thus forming two streams running at right angles to each other. These two streams are the result of the antagonistic vibratory impulses. Thus we have the introduction of the Law of Opposites moving right and left, the principles of duality instead of that of unity, represented by the figure "2" instead of "1."

What is it that causes the Law of Opposites? What causes this dual motion; these two directions of vibration? It is due to the two principles in nature, the electro-magnetic differentiation. If there were only one principle undifferentiated, then there would be the continual circle, but when we have introduced these two principles, the electrical and magnetic, we have the positive and negative poles. These two principles move in opposite directions. Thus we have the LINE.

The LINE is really made up of atoms moving in a continuous stream, or it would be more proper to say, they move in two continuous streams, for they do not move from one end to the other, but from the center to both ends. The

THE LINE

Line is thus like the preacher's prayer, commences in the middle and goes both ways. It is the positive and negative principles. All life, all existence is the manifestation of these two forces.

The Sex principle is here represented by this line, the masculine and feminine operative throughout all nature as well as in the individual. Wherever we see straight lines of force we may know that we are observing the operation of the Law of Opposites. It is the great universal antagonism, the great controversy that is operative throughout all time and space, the antagonism between these two natural forces. The struggle expresses itself in two directions. We have here the extremes of good and evil. Good is that which unites; evil is that which separates. They are two principles working everywhere. Good is that principle in nature which makes for righteousness; evil is the reverse; but the Line illustrates the two directions and shows them to be simply the effects of motion in these two directions.

The natural consequence of all manifestation is expression. The Zoroastrian doctrine of the two principles, good and evil, is shown by the Line; the Ormuzd and Ahriman, the eternal principle of good and evil. But there is another point of Theology that is illustrated by the Line. In the old Zend religion when we go back far enough, we find that Ormuzd and Ahriman are both emanations from one being. Ahriman is not a creation of Ormuzd, but is co-eternal with him and they are both emanations from one source. Thus we have in the first Divine aspect neither good nor evil; there is no such thing as moral differentiation, but on the contrary the two are perfectly united in one, or rather are unmanifest, undifferentiated. We have in this first Divine aspect a being who is neither good nor evil. Now, he sends forth the good emanation which is Ormuzd, a being whose nature is essentially good. Ahriman on the contrary is another emanation whose nature is essentially evil. These are the two expressions of one and the self-same spirit. Those manifestations must express themselves through differentiation. Now, this doctrine is perfectly represented by the Line, for it has two emanations going forth from the circle, the circle being the principle of unity having no quality save and excepting that of circularity. When the two impulses are imparted we have the energy going forth, the two impulses—the two emanations; thus imparted we have the energy going forth, thus drawing out the circle into a line. The Line is simply the extension from the point in the middle and is capable of infinite extension. Good and evil may thus be developed *ad infinitum,* and yet the farther they go in their development the farther apart they become. We see the fallacy of the idea that one may become good by doing evil,—the doctrine of doing evil that good may result. Good can never result from evil for the reason that evil is traveling in a geometrically opposite direction to good. Thus the end of the line, which represents the point of development, is continually receding farther from the center. Thus the one who is doing evil, is going farther and farther from the one who is doing good. The Line does not describe a circle no matter how far it goes, but is continually lengthening at right angles to the other end. The eternal opposition is thus going on and all further manifestation must, in the nature of things, be dependent upon this opposition. Not only is this true of the one who is doing a good, but also an evil, for it must be borne in mind that good and evil are really Kosmic Principles. They are not simply actions. Actions are but the expression of these Kosmic Principles. The Gods, Ormuzd and Ahriman, are not persons, but personifications of natural powers. As such they are to be understood as being powers actually operative in nature, forces, energies in fact. They are in reality the electro-magnetic force expressing itself in the form of moral relations and in order to understand this connection it must always be borne in mind that the only real basis of morality or immorality is in the attitude toward that which is neither moral nor immoral, toward that which transcends all moral relations. This great mystery, the mystery of ethics, is thus solved in the LINE. It is not true that there is political ethics or utilitarian ethics or anything of that kind. The basis of ethics is shown to be the relation of the relative to the absolute. Were there no absolute code of ethics, there could be no ethical foundation, for everything relates to the undifferentiated, to the circle, the unity, the Divine Oneness.

THE LINE

When we come to consider this matter, we can understand why it is that there have been ethical systems galore and yet no unity, no agreement, no harmony. It is because they have failed to recognize the central principle of unity to the foundation for all expression. The relative must ever be viewed in relation to the absolute. Good and evil are, therefore, two kinds of forces operative in the universe, ever antagonistic and their antagonism is due to the fact they are the same force moving in two opposite directions under the impulse of the one principle in its twofold aspect.

Light and darkness, another pair of opposites, are simply two different kinds of motion. Darkness is not the absence of light any more than light is the absence of darkness. They are two kinds of vibration, they are at right angles to each other. Not that we are to understand that they move through space at right angles, for the Line applies to a great many more things than simply space. Wherever there are two motions at right angles they are represented by the Line and when we use the term right angles here, we simply mean two opposite aspects.

Paracelsus taught that darkness was due to the radiation of certain dark stars, which radiated darkness just as the ordinary stars radiate light and the fool scientists have supposed he meant what he said, that he meant literally to claim that there were stars radiating darkness. This shows how ridiculous it is for physicists to attempt to explain the teachings of mysteries. What Paracelsus meant was that darkness had a source quite as definite as light; that it was a positive quality and not a mere negative one. It is a radiation; that is, it is the expression of a certain motion and when we have come to realize this we will then understand why it is that darkness has its occult influence the same as light, that is, quite as definite as light, being just the reverse. Also we speak of spiritual darkness because it is the expression of the other end of the line than spiritual light. Spiritual light is not used simply as a term to represent good. It is good, and spiritual darkness, as the opposite of light or good, is positively evil. These expressions could not be otherwise. They perfectly illustrate the real truth concerning the matter.

OCCULT GEOMETRY

Heat and Cold, all those other opposites are seen to be merely opposing vibratory forces, vibration going in two different directions, thus becoming the source of the twofold manifestation, the course of emanation in this particular respect. When it acts in another way it becomes the Sex Principle, thus male and female constituting another aspect of emanation, another pair of opposites. When this becomes specialized in organic beings it becomes the Sex Energy and the means unto the perpetuation of the race.

Wherever we turn we see the expression of this twofold vibrating force, which is in fact, the Law of Opposites, the Electro-Magnetic, Positive and Negative principle, which principle is the cause of the dual activities of the universe, —the twofold aspect of the dual activities of the Universe. The twofold aspect of Nature is but the expression of the Law of Opposites, the Eternal Two, symbolized by the LINE. Here we have Nature not as a unit, but as a duality, as the positive and negative poles. This dual force emanating in two directions, thus becomes the means of extending the Unity *ad infinitum*.

Until the positive-negative, the electro-magnetic, differentiation by emanation begins, no other emanation can take place. This must be the first step in the direction of manifestation. Thus we have presented to us the beginning of creation by emanation. It is this that is symbolized by the LINE because it is the LINE.

LESSON III

THE TRIANGLE

The TRIANGLE symbolizes the Law of Balance, and is geometrically the equal of the Number "3." The Law of Opposites, in the Triangle, is balanced, thus making Deity. It is in this sense that it is said that in the trinity duality becomes unity,—the three in one, and one in three.

As we learned in the previous lesson, all force divides itself into the positive and negative, or rather the electrical and magnetic, which are mutually positive and negative. We have, then, first a positive and second a negative, expressing themselves in two directions of force. Vibrating in these two directions, the Line is produced, due to the repulsion of force from a central point going outward in two directions. As long as these two vibratory impulses are all that are operative, we have the Line, but there is a third, which is neuter, being neither positive nor negative, or more properly speaking, being both positive and negative. This becomes the balancing force, the binding, interlacing, attaching principle, which instead of repelling the two principles, forms the center, draws them in to the center. In one sense it is, therefore, true that this is really the negative principle, whereas, the other two are both positive, one being positively electrical and the other positively magnetic. This third is negative both to the electrical and to the magnetic.

The first and second are centrifugal, the third is centripetal. Thus we have this neuter principle, which is negative to both the electrical and the magnetic, which draws in everything to its center. In this way, we have the uniting of the two forces, their balancing in a common center, so that this union is made possible. When they unite in the common

OCCULT GEOMETRY

center, they thus accomplish the balancing of the other opposing forces, becoming one.

We have thus repeated in the divine name, the "Yod" being the electrical principle and "He" the magnetic principle. These two principles are thus in opposition, but the "Vau," a nail, an attachment, a fastening, unites the two, thus they become one.

Why does the Triangle symbolize this union, this interlacement? First, imagine a point emanating two opposing forces; one will go to the right, the other to the left, and, as a matter of fact, the right hand is the electrical and the left hand the magnetic pole in man and everything else. A current of electricity is streaming to the right and a current of magnetism to the left, from this common point, thus forming a line at right angles. Now, place another point opposite the central point of this line, but in advance of it, and some distance away, sufficiently far in advance of the line to equal the length of the line, because this is to be negatived to both these forces. The attractive power must be as great and no greater than is the repulsive power of the other point; thus you advance your balancing point far enough to equal the length of the line. It, therefore, attracts the force at the two ends of the line, with equal power. By reason of this attraction the force is deflected from the regular path and caused to flow in the direction of this attraction. We have, therefore, force flowing in right angles from the central point, deflected from this right angle path in such a way as to flow inward to a point corresponding to that point from whence it first flowed, in the right angled path, drawn to this point by reason of the attraction which is equal both for the electrical and the magnetic. Thus we have a perfect triangle formed by the activity of these three forces. The electrical and the magnetic are now united in one given point. We have the perfect Triangle, which therefore, symbolizes the Law of Balance, as being the balancing of the electrical and the magnetic principles. The eternal warfare between the pairs of opposites has ceased, a truce has been made between the two. It is for this reason that the Triangle has ever been employed to symbolize the Law of Balance, that is the balancing of the two antagonistic

THE TRIANGLE

principles. It is thus trinity in unity and unity in trinity. But it must not be understood that this is simply an arbitrary symbol, because whenever two forces unite in one, whenever the pairs of opposites come together, thus forming a unity, which is the result of the combination of those pairs of opposites, we have the Triangle formed.

As long as force does not manifest, it always operates in this triangular form. There are the two directions of force brought together again by reason of the uniting in the third principle, forming the Triangle. But, what is the cause of this attraction? Are we to understand that there is another force besides the electrical and magnetic, a force in nature apart from the eternal Law of Opposites? No, this would be an error. Nothing exists in all nature but the two principles, and the various manifestation of the same. There is no third principle to be postulated in the sense of the electrical and magnetic. There is, therefore, no attractive principle out here to produce the other point of the Triangle. What then is it that causes the two points or ends of the line to be so deflected as to come together, forming the Triangle. It is a law of physics that two electrical atoms, or molecules; or two magnetic atoms or molecules, or electrons, will repel, but an electrical and a magnetic atom, electron or molecule, will usually attract; therefore, the two forces are streaming forth, the electric flowing to the right, the magnetic to the left; the centrifugal force drives both currents outward, at the same time the electrical current has an affinity for the magnetic current and the magnetic for the electric. The tendency, therefore, is for the electrical to draw the magnetic to it, and the magnetic to draw the electric. At the same time, the atoms, or electrons in the current, by reason of their repulsive force, drive all those in advance of them still further onward. They cannot turn back because of the repulsion coming from those electrons behind them; thus a return to the central point is impossible. Not only is this true, but the centrifugal force itself will not permit them to return for the reason that it has an antipathy for the electrons and is driving them ever onward in this right angle path. To return the same way they came is impossible. It is likewise, impossible for them to travel on indefinitely, because of the mutual attraction of the two currents. As the centrifugal force drives them outward and the centripetal force drives them inward, they are, in the very nature of things, caused to deflect from their regular course—made to pass inward until they again meet in a point opposite that point from which they proceeded. Thus, we have the triangle formed as the inevitable result of the centrifugal and centripetal forces operating in the electrical and magnetic principles. These principles without a third, operate in harmony with the Law of Opposites and the Law of Balance as well. It is, therefore, a case of emanation from the opposite forces until the point is reached where the negative force becomes the stronger. At this point the negative force begins to draw them inward, but the positive force is strong enough to cause the point of union to be equidistant from the two ends and at the same time at a distance equal to twice the space of deflection in a single principle, forming the perfect triangle.

The Triangle, however, must not be conceived of as being simply triangular in shape. It is also a triangle in power, for the forces are absolutely equal. Its strength is the same, the two principles, electric and magnetic, being equally powerful, and uniting, so as to perpetuate the absolute balance without a superior, in fact, the entire universe is a triangle, for the two principles of the Divine Essence are emanated through the Divine Will reaching that outward point, or emanation where the force of will becomes less than the force of desire; the heart of God, there causes a return through this force of desire, the tartness, or harshness as Boehme terms it. Returning to God, the point is reached where the force coming inward, produces what Boehme terms the flash, growing out of the sting or prickle, where again, the force is thrown out. Thus we have the process of creation, involution and evolution, a perpetual triangle, the two forces being driven outward and then drawn inward, through the twofold force, Will and Desire, until unity is reached. When unity has been reached it becomes positive, reverses the process, causing the forces to flow outward positively until Desire has become stronger than Will, when it returns again. Thus we have the triangle ever reversing itself. We have here the explanation of cycles of involution

THE TRIANGLE

and evolution.

It has been known to metaphysicians and mystics in all ages, that the processes of the universe are through cycles of involution and evolution. It is not a gradual process, but a cycle where every tendency is emanative, followed by one where everything is expressive of the return. One cycle represents the descent of spirit into matter, the next, the rise of matter into spirit. This problem is solved by the triangle. The Spirit's descent into matter is when the Will of God is emanating creation. The evolution of matter into spirit is when the Heart of God is drawing all things inward. Thus Manvantara and Pralaya are shown to be perfectly true by the Triangle,—Manvantara being the positive Will of God,—Pralaya being the negative Heart of God. These two forces do not act antagonistically so much as alternately, although, of course, they are both active, but on alternate days one is stronger than the other. A day of Brahma is shown to be the period when the Will is the heart plus;—Pralaya is when it is the heart minus. It is another illustration of the world old problem of the fatal children destroying their parents, for it is only by reason of the work achieved by the positive will that it becomes so weakened that the negative desire is able to overcome it, and when the negative desire has accomplished its purpose, it is then overcome by the positive will. Each accomplishes its work and by reason of this fact is so weakened as to become subject to the greater dominance of the other principle.

The eternal Triangle is, therefore, the form, both physically and metaphysically expressed, of the great struggle between Will and Desire, the struggle between the positive and negative principles. The Triangle is expressed in the Spirit of God, in the Divine Essence. For this reason we have the three principles in the Divine Essence. Again we find it in the Universal Spirit, expressing itself through Brahma, or the Creative Force;—Shiva, or the destructive force,—Vishnu, or the binding, uniting force; the perfect blending and harmonizing of the two, producing harmony, balance. Again in nature, we find the trinity expressing itself through electricity and magnetism united in the creation which is the expression of both.

OCCULT GEOMETRY

We have in man the Human Triangle on all the planes of nature expressed as electricity and magnetism, the positive and negative force, with the uniting of the two expressed in the human soul.

Thus we have the Divine Triangle, the Spiritual Triangle, the Kosmic Triangle, and the Human Triangle. It is for this reason that the Trinity has from time immemorial been recognized by occult scientists, as the key to all the mysteries; not the Trinity of the Father, Son and Holy Ghost, but the Trinity of the three principles in each and every being.

The Number 3, is, therefore, the Masonic principle; the number of the perfect man as the one containing in himself the two principles united. Thus we have in the Triangle the Law of Opposites involving all the ten pairs of opposites, united and unified in the Law of Balance. It being a perfect Triangle, that is, all its three lines being equal, we should understand that unity is as dependent upon one of these forces as upon the other. One is just as necessary as the other. By applying the Triangle to the ten pairs of opposites, we will be able to form a Triangle for each of them; letting the positive one represent the electrical principle, the negative the magnetic, establish this state of mutual attraction and thus draw out a point where the two become one. You will in this way have formed the Triangle of which Light and Darkness are the two extremes; also one of which the two extremes are good and evil; dry and wet; hot and cold; stationary and moving; square and oblong; male and female; and so on with all the other pairs of opposites. They will represent the two points of opposition, and the harmonizing point between, the union, the marriage between the opposites, for the Triangle simply means the marriage of the two opposites, resulting in unity.

LESSON IV

THE CROSS

The CROSS has from time immemorial, been associated with the idea of Sex differentiation, among Mystics, and also for a very long time, with the idea of sacrifice. It did not originate with the crucifixion of Jesus, but existed long ages previous. It was in its origin a Phallic Symbol, representing the reproductive process, the process of human generation, and as such was used by the Romans as the means of execution, symbolizing as it did the greatest ignomity, because one was put out of life through the Cross by which he entered life,—thus signifying that it was a mistake that he was ever born, that he should never have been born—thus he is put out of life on the Cross, the symbol of Generation. It was thus used to symbolize the extinction of that which was generated.

After the crucifixion of Christ, because it had extinguished the human in Him, it was employed by the Christian Mystics to symbolize the extinction of everything which is the product of human generation, in order that that spiritual element which is imparted by initiation, may survive.

But it is important that we should know what is involved in this Phallic Symbol. It is the masculine and feminine unity, the Cross of the two, in a sense; but why is this particular form introduced to symbolize the two principles? Because it is the perfect expression of the truth in regard to this separation.

The earlier form of the Cross does not have the upper portion. The Egyptian Tau is one of the first forms.

To illustrate the principle involved, suppose we draw a perpendicular line, which will represent the one force advancing from the starting point; in other words, it is the emanation of one principle, the bi-sexed emanation. In time we have this current of force, represented by the Line, parting, so the line opens, becoming two converging lines at right angles. Thus we have the right hand electrical and the left hand magnetic lines flowing outward, forming the primitive Cross which is roughly represented by the Egyptian Tau, the first form of the Cross, that which originated before the idea of crucifixion. The Cross in this form is the symbol representing a current of force parting and thus flowing in two opposite directions. We should not suppose that this is merely a current, for as a matter of fact, the current really does part and flow in just this way. It is the twofold masculine and feminine emanation coming out from the single bi-sexed emanation. Thus the Cross is the perfect symbol of the manifesting force, masculine and feminine. Creation by emanation is consequently the separation of the one principle into the two principles, these two principles, masculine and feminine. In other words, the separation through sex differentiation, is the source of manifestation, thus the descent of the Spirit into matter is made possible. All manifestation must necessarily be through sex differentiation, through the separation of the two principles. It follows, therefore, that the return or the evolution of the Spirit, the forward cycle of progress must be through the polarization of the two principles and their return into unity, thus turning back the current, stopping the process of emanation and causing the forces to flow into the one center.

Life is brought about through the separation of the two principles, likewise does death result from the same cause. Life in this form must terminate in death. To solve the mystery of the Cross, is to polarize the two principles until they become one.

The race of men as we know it, is the product of the Cross, of the separation of the Sexes. The uniting of the two principles in one would mean the destruction of the present form of life and the introduction of a new order of beings. We read in the Bible in the common version,—"And about this time began men to call upon the name of the Lord," but this is a gross translation. A literal rendering of the Hebrew

THE CROSS

is, "And about this time began men to call by the name Jehovah." In plain English, about this time men began to call themselves Jehovah. Jehovah is the Rabbinical form of the ineffable name, "Yod-He-Vau-He;" therefore, about this time men began to call themselves by the ineffable name. This undoubtedly refers to an assumption on their part of having in themselves the character of "Yod-He-Vau-He." They were liars, else they would not have died. They were assuming the prerogative of the Eternal without having embodied His keynote. Jehovah means the everlasting one. It is the term translated "Eternal," in the Hebrew Scriptures. The "Yod" is the male principle; the "He" is the feminine principle of the Divine Essence. The "Vau" or Vow, is the attachment, the link which unites the two, the neuter principle, in which the duality becomes trinity, thus merging into unity; thus becoming the separated sex principle united in one, the second "He" the opening, representing the expulsion through the womb of creation, emanation. Thus, by calling themselves Jehovah, men were assuming to have this relation established in themselves, namely, the perfect polarization of the "Yod" with the "He" so that all distinction was lost, they becoming perfectly balanced. In this way they would be able to generate the new creation, not the manifesting universe, not God, but the higher principle in themselves; thus life everlasting would come through the polarization of the Sex principle.

It is the Lingam completely merged in the Yoni. In this case the Yoni indeed and in truth as manifested through the generation of offspring, but the door of the higher life, Aeonian life.

The solving of the mystery of the Cross is the crucifixion of the manifest life in order that the unmanifest may be made possible. Crucifixion is, therefore, the destruction of that which is represented by the Cross, the turning inward instead of outward of the two sex principles. It is thus the nailing of one on the Cross.

The other form of the Cross, the one most familiar to us, namely a horizontal intersecting a perpendicular, represents the crossing of the two principles, the horizontal being the symbol of flowing water, the great deep, which is the symbol of substance, the feminine aspect of the creative act, therefore, the feminine or magnetic principle, the Yoni. The upright, is the Phallic, the Lingam, intersecting the Yoni. In other words, it is the electrical or masculine principle, penetrating substance. We have thus the active and passive crossing; the intersection of the two, the positive and negative, crossing force. In this aspect of the Cross we have the mystery of creation presented from another standpoint; not from the standpoint of sexual differentiation, but from that of the crossing of the passive principle by the active. Why is the horizontal placed at the upper end of the upright instead of the center in this form of the Cross? Obviously because it is intended to represent the passing of the upright through the horizontal, the passing of energy through force. It, therefore, does not represent the two as passive, as static thus maintaining the same relation, but the feminine as static, and the masculine as dynamic. In this way we have the dynamic principle passing through the static showing the energizing or substance as the source of creation.

The Cross, has, therefore, from time immemorial been associated with the idea of sex differentiation as the first step in creation by emanation and also with that of the energizing of substance as the means of generating life and form and as has been stated, the putting to death upon the Cross was an insult implying that it was a mistake that one was ever generated; that he should be thrown back into the state of non-existence, should be reduced into the form of passive substance in the sense of contrast with active energy, —thus the work of the Cross of Life, is to be reversed by the Cross of Death.

In its mystical application it means first the destruction of this earthly creation, of emanation, of obliteration of that which has sprung forth, the reduction of the product of physical generation into the limbo of non-existence, and at the same time the energizing of substance with the Divine force in order to its transmutation into the higher substance, resulting in the germination of the Divine Life. When we realize the nature of the creative act we see that the Cross is the perfect symbol for the representation of this activity. Nothing could so perfectly symbolize both the physical and

THE CROSS

spiritual generation as well as the destruction absolutely and the destruction of the physical as a means of ushering in the spiritual, as the Cross.

The Maltese Cross is a still better symbol of creation by emanation, but representing the emanation in four directions, being rather the symbol of the second "He" the emanation through the Triad, thus having practically the same meaning as the Swastika.

As the Cross broadens toward the ends, we are to understand the diffusion of the force as it passes on. As it goes outward it is continually manifesting on a broader scale. It is thus the emanation of the universe from one point where the two principles cross. This cross has no relation to the crucifixion of Christ and, in fact, all the forms of the cross were Phallic Symbols either natural or mystical until they were clarified by the solving of the problem of the cross, by the Great Master, Jesus, who thus became Master of the Cross of generation and was able to dominate the creative force henceforth.

The Cross as a Christian symbol represents the crucifixion of the man as a preparation for the resurrection, clarification of the Christ man, and when used to symbolize this it is simply applying the very same principles, the very same activity and chemical constitution as is manifested in the activity of the electro-magnetic principle in all nature, for this is exactly the way the forces do move, in regard to the first form of the Cross, the right hand and left hand movement. It should be borne in mind that the electrical principle does flow to the right hand circle, energizing substance in its revolution;—the right hand path is, therefore, the true Path of all energy and we see in all the manifested, the right hand as the masculine ever, and the left hand as the feminine. The Cross being made as the electrical principle flows from the left side of the brain to the right hand nerves and the magnetic principles from the right hand side of the brain to the left hand nerves, thus we have even in man the crossing of the two principles. The secret of regeneration is by crossing them the second time so that the two principles are united, becoming one. The cross is thus used to symbolize this process in nature, because the process

OCCULT GEOMETRY

is a Cross, because it does actually make the sign of the Cross, in all its activities, the sign of the Cross being the physical action, the sexual differentiatory emanation. It is, therefore, used to symbolize that which really takes this form; but more than this we cannot say. The deeper spiritual mysteries of the Cross must be concealed. They can be uttered only by the aeraphary at low breath, from mouth to ear, therefore, we must refrain from imparting any further information on the subject at this time or in this way.

LESSON V

THE SWASTIKA

The SWASTIKA is the Cross of India. It is the form employed by the Hindus and is the Sign of Pisces in the Indian Zodiac.

The Swastika is a cross formed of two lines crossing in the middle, making a four arm cross, with the ends of the cross bent back at right angles to the arms; thus we have the suggestion of a square.

The Swastika is intended to represent four streams of energy flowing from a common point in four opposite directions. Thus we have the positive and negative, the electrical and magnetic forces going in four opposite directions geometrically, but when we realize that the four elements of the alchemists, Earth, Water, Fire, Air, are the products of the four streams of forces, then we will understand that the four directions do not refer to physical geometry, but rather to the four fields of matter, the four orders of divisions of the physical world. The two lines cross; thus we have the upright, symbolizing the electrical principle, and the horizontal, representing the magnetic. These cross in the center and this cross is really the point from which the four streams flow out. We have thus the electrical which goes forward and downward, the positive electric becoming the element of fire or the luminiferous ether which afterwards becomes oxygen gas; the negative becomes the element of water or the gustiferous ether or hydrogen gas. The positive magnetic becomes the earth element, carbon, or the odoriferous ether, and the negative magnetic air, nitrogen, or tangiferous ether. We have these four ethers, the four lower Tattvas, the four elements of the old alchemists, the four elemental gases, nitrogen, oxygen, hydrogen and carbon, as the common emanations from one point. The Swastika, therefore, represents these four as the emanations from the one common center, the one point. The electrical and magnetic are flowing from this point to their two poles. Thus we have this central point of separation as the Sonoriferous Ether, which is electro-magnetism in its united state, also contained in the ether.

We have thus in the Swastika the upper triad of physical matter, ether, electricity and magnetism, dividing itself into the four currents which become the four lower Tattvas. The Higher Tattva, the Sonoriferous Ether, is dividing itself into the four lower Tattvas and streaming forth into the four regions. This is also represented by the second "He" in the ineffable name, the "Yod" being the masculine, the first "He" the feminine and the "Vau" the attachment, the binding, the union, interlacement, thus forming the Trinity. The second "He" is the opening of that trinity into expression—symbolizing an opening—the womb from which is born the Universe. In the same way, the Swastika symbolizes emanation from the Trinity. It is the Trinity represented in the Central point flowing out in the four arms.

Thus we have here the four elements of the Alchemists as the fourfold emanation of the Trinity within. The question then is, why are the ends of the Swastika bent backwards?— Because the Swastika is a wheel of fire. It is not conceived of as standing still, but as a wheel continually revolving. The fire refers to its electro-magnetic character. As the wheel revolves, the force of the revolution overcomes the force of the stream, the strength of the rush. The result is the stream of fire is deflected from its regular course being bent back in a direction opposite the one in which the wheel is traveling. Thus we have the ends of the arms of the cross bent backward. The revolution shows us that it was a whirl, describing a circle, and as we have previously learned, all energy travels in whirls. The result is, it is not simply this fourfold emanation that is to be taken into consideration. The Swastika does not stop at emanating the four principles but they are emanated in an active state. Action is going on all the time of the emanation. The four principles are

THE SWASTIKA

active after having emanated. Thus they go forth and produce other forms of matter as well.

The circular revolution means the revolution around a given point, the circling of energy around a nucleus, which is the secret of creation. As force continually circles around a common nucleus, it revolves and gathers up, thus generating a common nucleus. All forms are generated through the circular action which gathers substance around a nucleus. We have, therefore, in this revolving wheel of Fire, the means of creation. Thus the world below these four elements is produced by their revolution. In other words, the ninety-two so-called elements are the effects of the revolution of this wheel of fire. As it continually circles, they are gathered up, generated and thrown off, that is, the molecules of those diverse elements. Thus we have the physical world as we see it, as the effect of their evolution of the wheel of fire. By this revolution we simply mean its activity. The action of the wheel of fire is thus responsible for the generation of the forms of creation which presents themselves to our vision.

There are two forms of the Swastika; one represents the wheel of fire revolving to the right, thus the arms bent backward to the left; the other represents the Swastika revolving to the left, and thus the arms bent back to the right. The right hand Swastika, that is the one with the arms bent to the left, is the true Swastika, representing the constructive principle of nature. The left hand Swastika, the one with the arms bent to the right is the destructive principle, the left hand path, energy going to the left and, therefore, destroying, disintegrating. The one is the principle of creation, the other of destruction. The one represents the centripetal, the other the centrifugal principle. The right hand Swastika, therefore, is the symbol of Kosmic creation, while the left hand Swastika is the symbol of Kosmic destruction.

But why does the Swastika take this form, with the arms bent at right angles to their general course, thus suggesting a square, instead of a curving gradually to form a circle. The reason is because this is the result of four streams revolving with great force and at the same time rushing forward. They are thus made to bend back at right angles because the two movements are about equal. The square turn, however, is really suggestive of another point, namely, the fact that all these principles that are emanated in the Universe are the products of these four elements. They can all be reduced to the four elements; they do not become a circle entirely indivisible, but rather represent a square, showing the four principles in their various mutations, and everywhere in the universe we find the presence of the positive electric and magnetic forces. We can never get rid of this classification no matter how near the surface we approach. The manifest universe is, consequently a square, it is the square of the triangle and in this we have a suggestion of the problem of the squaring of the circle.

But not only does the Swastika operate on the physical plane; in a certain sense it operates on all the planes of nature; for we have the same positive and negative electromagnetic differentiation in the Desire World. Thus we have the Desire Swastika or Astral Swastika, having the same meaning as the physical Swastika only it is applied to Desire Stuff.

The Swastika of Desire is the upper desire Trinity differentiating itself into the four lower notes making a square. The square and the triangle thus form the septenary of the heart; and on the Mental Plane likewise, we have the mental triangle forming the region of abstract thought, the square or Swastika of the mind, corresponding to the region of concrete thought. The Mental body is the same as the Swastika, while the Causal body is the triangle above, the point from which emanation takes place. The Buddhic Swastika has the same relation to Buddhi, representing the four lower notes of the Buddhic octave and showing the radiation from the three higher notes, representing the Buddhic triangle; and the same is true of the Spiritual triangle and the Spiritual Swastika.

The Swastika is, therefore, the electrical and magnetic principles positively and negatively polarized, going forth into activity. It is the manifestation of the higher trinity which represents the undifferentiated principle and its electro-magnetic differentiation before those two principles have divided into their respective poles. On all the planes of

THE SWASTIKA

nature, therefore, we find the Swastika. It is prominently the symbol of the quarternary; as the emanation of the triad, the two forming the septenary.

In another sense we may use the four lower principles of nature as the gross physical body, the Etheric or Vital and the Kama as the Swastika emanating from the Trinity consisting of Atma, Buddhi and Manas.

The Swastika is likewise a symbol of Sex because it represents the masculine and feminine principles divided into the positive and negative. Thus there is positive and negative masculinity flowing forth and positive and negative femininity from the other center, the two Sex principles thus sending forth their positive and negative forces giving rise to all affinities in life. Sex is thus seen to be a Kosmic principle, not simply an individual one. The individual but embodies the Kosmic sex principles. Having embodied that he expresses it in such a way as to become positive to certain forces and negative to others. It is thus through the working of the Sexual Swastika that love and hate are brought into operation. We love certain ones by reason of those sexual affinities; others we hate because of the sexual antipathies. The Swastika is thus the emblem of sex differentiation and shows those four principles to be merely mutations on one principle as they all flow from one common center.

The Swastika is preeminently, therefore, the symbol of creation by emanation. Thus as the triangle represents the Law of Opposites and the Law of Balance, resulting in unity, so the Swastika, represents the fourfold emanation of the Universe coming out from unity, and differentiation growing out of unity,—thus the Universe emanating from God. The Swastika is the symbol of the manifested universe acting both creatively and destructively from the one point, which is the same as the Circle of Fire streams forth the four positive forces in one sense positive and negative, but in the sense of flowing from one point, all positive, which go forth to create.

Why is the Swastika used as a symbol, a talisman, in some instances? Because it represents these principles and it is used talismanically for the express purpose of sending forth corresponding forces. When chemically used, it is the means

OCCULT GEOMETRY

unto the creation of new forms of energy. But why is it used to represent the sign Pisces? Because Pisces, the feet, is the lowest part of the Grand Solar Man, signifying the final emanation of force, representing the last principle of the manifested Universe. Pisces is the same to the Grand Solar Man as Swastika is to the Universe. The Swastika being understood, its meaning being known, was used by the Hindus to symbolize Pisces in order that we might understand the esoteric meaning of the Sign. The fishes do not correctly give its meaning, but when we understand the Swastika we have a key to the meaning of that sign, for it is the same.

Again, we find that the Swastika was the discuss of both Sankaracharya and Krishna. It is, in fact, the discuss employed by every Avatar of Vishnu, as a weapon. When you realize that it means these two directions of force, both creation and destruction, thus symbolizing the creative and destructive principles of nature, hurling of the discuss means simply that the Avatar of Vishnu is master of the creative and destructive principles of nature in Kosmic as well as in individual life. It was to symbolize these truths that the Swastika was employed.

LESSON VI

THE DIAMOND

The DIAMOND is really formed by the union of two triangles pointing at right angles. It thus means the triangle operative in two directions. The two triangles generally mean the individual and the Kosmic triangles, the microcosm and the macrocosm. The Microcosm is described by the upper triangle, being the rising from the base, the electromagnetic principles forming the base, rising to the point of union midway between the points and above them, forming a triangle, which ever rises upward. The correct position for the individual triangle is that of perfect union with the Kosmic triangle; that is to say, the individual triangle should be swallowed up in the Kosmic and lose itself there.

The Diamond represents just the reverse, the individual triangle pointing downward, beginning at its base on the base line of the Kosmic triangle and pointing in the opposite direction. It is, therefore, seen that every step taken in the direction of individual development, every step taken in the development of the individual, is a step away from Kosmic harmony. In exact proportion as we develop our own triangle, as we balance the two forces in ours, and thus develop self-centeredly, we are removed from a state of Kosmic harmony. It will, therefore, be seen that Kosmic Consciousness and individualism are absolute antipodes. There is no trace of harmony between the two conceptions. The individual is going away from the state of Kosmic harmony.

Further, you will notice that the Kosmos in its triangle ever rises upward. By the mere union of the two forces elevation becomes essential, for the electro-magnetic forces are so far apart as the universe is large; that is, those forces travel to the utmost bounds of the universe, therefore, their polarization must, in the very nature of things lift them to the highest point of the universe. One by uniting himself, or rather losing his Individual Triangle, in the Kosmic Triangle, will thus be elevated to the highest point of natural achievement. It is for this reason that when the individuality is completely surrendered the highest possible attainment is reached. Para-Nirvana is simply the bringing of the individual triangle into perfect union with the universal so that they become one, but in the Diamond symbol this has not been the case. The individual triangle has not been swallowed up in the universal, but in fact, has severed itself and is going in a direction exactly opposite to that of the Kosmic Triangle. It is the individual life rather than the Kosmic Life, consequently the man is going in a direction opposite that of the Kosmic Force. What does this mean? Evidently that man in his search for knowledge does not polarize himself with the universal force and allow it to communicate its message to him, which is the natural order, but rather seeks to find out things in his own way. It is not intended by nature that man should find out anything but rather that he shall become the channel through which nature shall reveal herself. "As above, so below; as below, so above." Man is the microcosm of the Universe. Every principle of man is in everything else; every principle of the Universe is in man. This being the case, it logically follows that if a man will perfectly polarize his principles with the corresponding principles in nature and become negative, he being the negative pole and nature the positive pole, the principles of nature will illuminate the principles of his own being. His soul will thus receive the message through the diverse principles of the universe and he will thus receive Truth statically. This was the case with Paracelsus, he knew scarcely anything, but divined almost everything. Paracelsus did not use the ordinary methods of research, he did not find out so much from laboratory experimentation, although he did quite a good deal of it, he did not learn from books; he did not acquire knowledge through experience and observation in the way that many consider it necessary to acquire it now; but he rather divined the truth, and his experiments were not so much to find out as to verify what he had already divined. He was a man who was inspired by Nature. This is what he means by "reading the Open Book of Nature." Let Nature reveal herself. When Nature reveals herself to man, he being negatively polarized with her, will know absolute Truth. This is the true method of investigation. It is not to experiment, but to contemplate and when one has learned to contemplate Nature and to depend upon his intuition, he will have found that which is absolutely reliable. This course will cause him to be drawn up into union with the Kosmos. The Kosmic Union must necessarily result from a course of contemplation upon the Universe,—the making of Gnana Yoga, as the Yogi term it; but the man who has not learned to do this, but prefers to inspect the different parts of Nature, in an impractical manner, has turned his back upon the course of Nature. He is not trying to be swallowed up in Nature, but rather to bring Nature unto his own measure, to test Nature and weigh her in the balance and find out just what goes to constitute her. But this is impossible. Any fool ought to know that he is unable to weigh Nature in any such manner. We have the story of Augustine, who one day when he was meditating upon the Universe, upon the eternal, saw a child who was sitting by the seaside, dipping up water and putting it in a hole. He asked the child what he was doing and he answered, "I am emptying the ocean into this hole." "Well you cannot do that, my child," and the child says, "Neither can you contain the universe in your mind." The child was really an angel in disguise, come to teach Augustine that lesson. The scientist should realize this lesson, namely, the inability of man to bring the Kosmos into his recognition through the ordinary methods of investigation, and the necessity of his being swallowed up in the Kosmos. Augustine could not contain the universe in his mind, but his mind could be quite readily swallowed up in the Universe. Even so, man cannot investigate the universe,—he can only interrogate it. This should not be taken to mean that it is impossible for us to know absolute Truth, as this assumption would be an error. It simply shows us that the inductive method of research is absolutely incapable of bringing us into a realization of absolute Truth. The Diamond thus represents this method of investigation, which cannot lead to a realization of the harmony of the Universe, but must ever go in the opposite direction, thus taking man away from harmony and causing him to realize only the phenomenal aspect of things and only that portion which he will be able to cognize through his senses.

Again, the Diamond is the hardest of all stones, the fartherest removed from fluidity, the state of flux necessary to qualify one to receive impressions with the greatest ease. It, therefore, symbolizes the crystallizing influence of impractical research and individualistic activities, its tendency to drive all elements together, to crystallize in one point and prevent one from responding to the impulse coming from Nature, and in fact, this perfectly represents the tendency of all positive research. The true position of the investigator, as has been before stated, is one of negative polarization with the Kosmos, but the positive attitude works in just the reverse direction. When one is negatively polarized, that is in a receptive attitude in relation to the Kosmos, he will thus be impressed by all the operations of the Kosmos. He will listen to the Song of Life and the Music of the Spheres. He will sense all those forces from without and therefore, get a glimpse beyond the threshold of those things. He will know what is going on in the Universe, by reason of his divining faculty. He will thus become a prophet of science. But the man who starts out to find everything in his own way, who does not ask of the Universe, who proposed to conquer it, who treats it not as an intelligent being, but as a mechanical structure, recognizing only the idea of mechanical uniformitarianism, shuts himself out from all those things, and therefore, he does not respond and does not know anything excepting what he can learn through the use of the five physical senses and such instruction as will aid those senses. His knowledge being confined absolutely to the physical, he is hardened so that he is unable to respond to the vibrations of the higher planes of nature, therefore, he does not know anything beyond the physical plane.

Another suggestion is the fact that the Diamond cuts whatever it comes in contact with. Even so, our materialistic

THE DIAMOND

investigator cuts his way through Nature. If he finds any part of nature that does not agree with his materialistic conceptions, casts it away instead of embodying it. He recognizes only that part of nature which happens to be in harmony with his own hypothesis.

You will observe that the Diamond in the form in which it is usually represented, is pointing upward and downward. The individual triangle will, therefore, be pointing downward, and you will notice our scientific investigator is always delving in the ground, he never looks upward, never polarizes himself with the universe, the Divine, in order that he may know the Truth, but is ever delving in that which is below the surface, ever looking in the earth, for the source of everything, and this is found to be literally true, for the biologists generally think they will find the source of life and of all things in the physical state of matter. They delve in the sea and discover the germs of life. They banish the God of Heaven and have enthroned the God of protoplasm. This conception of the scientists makes it an utter impossibility for him to ever acquire any real Truth,—Truth and the scientific method are absolutely irreconcilable. Our scientist so long as he follows the idea of physical causation and searches to discover truth, so long as he runs after truth instead of inviting truth to come to him, must ever be thrown off the track. The Diamond perfectly symbolizes this attitude, namely the fact that the investigator is turned away from the real course of the universe. The Universe finds its balancing point in God, that which is above. The two opposites are balanced in God, the point of emanation. Man must likewise find his balancing point in God as the point of emanation, and recognize this as the fundamental principle of his philosophy, if he would bring himself into harmony with the universe, but he does not do this; he turns his balancing point to the earth, to the very lowest point, and thus the Law of Balance is in no way recognized, for from the failure to recognize the Law of Opposites and the Law of Balance as well as the Doctrine of Emanations, it becomes utterly impossible for a man to know the Truth.

The Diamond is found in the blue clay in the earth and so we find man ever delving in the earth instead of rising into the clouds; ever going on in the dust, never striving to rise above it, to transcend all of these material limitations. He is always fixing his attention on materiality and, therefore, he does not rise to that which is the source of the physical, keeping himself ever in the physical.

The Diamond is crystallized carbon, and the individual when he realizes his true nature will realize that he is but the crystallization of the forces of Nature; that his individuality is an illusion. That is, certain natural forces have been brought to bear upon the diverse kinds of matter and thus man has become but the crystallization of those various elements and is in no sense of the world, an entity separate and apart from the various natural elements. He is the crystallization of Nature, but has his back turned to Nature. Instead of realizing his identity with Nature and thus the possibility of finding Nature within his own soul, the possibility of looking within and finding Nature there, he has turned his back upon Nature, supposing that he can conquer her.

The Law of Correspondences makes it possible for man to study Nature by a process of analogy; that is, to study himself and take man as a symbol of the universe, finding the correspondence between the diverse attributes of his own being and the diverse attributes of Nature, thus finding in himself the microcosm of the universe. He neglects this—repudiating the Law of Correspondences altogether and considers Nature not as a great world of which he is the little world, not as his larger self, but as a mechanical uniformitarian arrangement which is to be studied by himself. You will see, therefore, that he really regards himself as being superior to Nature. Nature is, to him, a mechanical arrangement, a machine which is totally devoid of intelligence; he considers that man is the only intelligent being, the only one, therefore, who can understand anything. He takes a positive instead of a negative attitude and is, therefore, not teachable; Nature cannot teach him anything. He undertakes to do everything himself. The result is Nature remains a sealed book to him. He becomes the Diamond or rather, one point of the Diamond, and here we have the other triangle, representing the other end of the Diamond

THE DIAMOND

and you will notice that the other end of the Diamond is hard just as human nature is.

Nothing can cut the Diamond. What does this mean? Simply the great truth that no man by such method has ever found out any truth, has never learned anything about Nature; he cannot cut through her; he cannot penetrate her. She is an adamant to all his attacks, therefore, by this positive method he never has and never will learn a single thing about Nature. She stands as a wall against all his efforts.

Again, the Diamond is found in the earth, which in the Kosmic Triangle signifies that by such methods one will never be able to see anything but the earthly, material side of Nature. By such kind of investigation she appears to be only a manifestation of mechanical uniformitarianism; her higher principles elude all his search. Further, she is always kept at the opposite extreme from him. This method will never bring one to a realization of Nature. Nature is always the great enigma. The riddle of the universe is unsolved only because man tries to solve it positively instead of negatively. The Diamond thus signifies the scientific mind and the unsolvable nature of the universal problem when attacked from this standpoint.

Another thing to be noticed is that the two triangles do not represent the base line, they present only the angular lines running from the corners to the point. There is no cross line in the middle. This signifies that man and nature are not separate but are two aspects of one and the same thing. The Kosmic triangle represents the macrocosm and the individual triangle the microcosm. They are one and the same. The Kosmic triangle is the sum total of the universe, while the individual triangle is the particular manifestation of that universe. Man's ignorance is the result of his failure to realize this great truth. It is because he thinks he is an individual instead of a manifestation of the universe that he is not able to accomplish anything. The whole illusion, the blinding forces is due to man's following the illusion. When he once loses this and attains the consciousness of his unity with Nature, the whole enigma is solved.

The Diamond, therefore, teaches us the way by which this Maya can be made to give place to absolute Truth.

OCCULT GEOMETRY

Another point in the symbol is the great reflective power of the Diamond. The Diamond becomes a miniature Sun, gathering up the rays of light and reflecting them. There is no other gem in the world that is such a perfect mirror of light as the Diamond. This should teach us that all the truth which man can learn is merely that which is reflected in him through the universe. No man is an originator of anything. He is merely a mirror in which the Kosmos is reflected and the wisest man is simply the most efficient mirror. As he comes more into harmony with the Universe as a mirror he gets brighter, so that the Universe is able to reflect herself in him more effectively. The highest development to which we attain, merely fits us for a still higher efficiency as a reflecting instrument. Thus the Kosmos is reflected in us and we are thus able to understand it.

Furthermore, the universal triangle is but a reflection of God, having no identity in itself, being merely a reflection of the Divine perfection. Thus when we look into the face of nature we see the reflection of the Divine. When man has learned this, the great Kosmic enigma, the riddle of the universe will have disappeared, will have been solved, it will then be made plain to him.

The Diamond presents to us the attitude of man and nature at the present time. The problem for man to solve if he would attain to absolute truth, is to reverse the position of his triangle relative to the universal triangle. We see this problem in the Hexagram when the individual triangle is lifted so that the two are interlaced. Man should lift it up and change his nature, until it exactly coincides with the Kosmic Triangle.

Another aspect of the Diamond is in the arrangement of the material and spiritual triangles in man; that is, the three lower principles, the Kama Rupa, the Linga Sharira and the Prana, the two physical and the vital principles, representing the lower triangle, pointing in exactly the opposite direction from Atma, Buddhi, Manas being the Spiritual Triangle, while Kama, the Desire Nature, is the point of separation where the two unite. We see thus man's desires going downward to the earth in opposition to his aspirations which go forward to heaven. Because of these two direc-

THE DIAMOND

tions, because of the antagonism of the desires and aspirations, the confusion in the individual life is forever present. We can see the two forces working in the individual which prevent him from rising. This problem can be solved only by the swallowing up of the desires in the aspirations. Not only is this true of the individual, however, but the Diamond represents in another sense, the slow course of Nature, the upward and downward tendencies, the two forces acting in direct opposition to each other. Until man has solved this problem, has overcome the antagonism, he cannot unite with Nature, and until Nature has come into harmony with God, until the outflowing tendency has entirely given place to the return, she will be unable to fulfill her destiny. The Diamond is thus a picture of things as they are, representing man in his rebellion against God, picturing the condition of the fall both of the universe and man. The two ends of the Diamond must be reversed and brought together, so that they will exactly coincide, so that the material triangle will be completely swallowed up in the spiritual triangle, the individual in the Kosmic triangle, and the natural triangle in the Divine triangle. In this way the Universe will be the perfect expression of God, and man the perfect expression of the present embodiment of the universe, instead of being the condition of chaos presented at the present time.

These things are symbolized in the Diamond. It was to represent all these ideas of them, as the case might be, that the Diamond was adopted as a symbol, not only from the standpoint of its geometrical form, but also its chemical constitution. The very nature of the Diamond gives expression to this reflective principle as it operates throughout all Nature, therefore, it is used to symbolize the two triangles operating in opposition to each other.

LESSON VII

THE PENTAGRAM

One of the greatest symbols is the PENTAGRAM, the five-pointed star. This is a magical symbol of the greatest potency when correctly drawn with the four points forming a square and the fifth point in mid-heaven. In this way it is, to a certain extent, the symbol of Man, the two lower points representing the feet, the two middle points the arms and the upper point the head, while the body of the star will represent the body of Man. It is thus the symbol of Man. But again we find it symbolizing the Mental Body, the Manasic principle in general. Beginning at the bottom we have the Gross Body, the Magnetic Body, Prana and Kama as the four base principles on which the fifth or Manas rests. This star having five points symbolizes the five principles and thus represents the fifth, Manas rising above the other principles. To a certain extent, it is a symbol of the theory of evolution, a belief in man's evolving from the physical up to the spiritual, thus making Manas the fifth principle to be developed.

The position of the star indicates that the mind should rise above the other principles; should be in the ascendency; should be the keynote of the man, in fact.

When it is used as a Magical symbol it is employed for the purpose of attracting the Manas from around one or from the Kosmic and Mental Planes, to draw it down and thus enable one to employ it. Of course, the reason why it accomplishes this work in the performance of ceremonial magic is because by looking on it or by drawing it, one forms in mind a picture of this five-pointed star, and as this form exactly corresponds to Manas, in fact, is the hieroglyph of

THE PENTAGRAM

Manas, the Mental vibration will be set up in one's Aura, that is, the vibration of the Mental Body will be stimulated in a high degree, and as those vibrations are stimulated the activity of the Mental Body will be raised. One will thus become intensely active in the mental sense. As one becomes mentally active he will draw to himself the Manas from the Mental Plane, becoming thus the focal point for the activity of this Manas; his Mental Body becoming a nucleus around which will be gathered the Manas. It is in this way that the drawing of the Pentagram or the gazing upon it, will be the means of greatly intensifying the Manasic power in the performance of ceremonial magic. It is not necessary that one should know the relation of the Pentagram to Manas in order to employ it in this way, though, of course, such knowledge will be of inestimable value as it will greatly increase the potency of the act, for the Pentagram is the form which Manas takes in its activity. It is the natural symbol, the natural figure and, therefore, visualizing upon it will naturally stimulate the Manasic activity.

What is said in reference to the Mental Body is also true of the Kosmic Manas. The realm of gross matter and the etheric region will represent the two lower points. The next higher will represent Prana diffused throughout the Universe and the Kama or desire stuff. Manas will be the highest point. Therefore, the five-pointed star will symbolize the five lower principles of the universe; in other words the physical, astral and mental worlds. These three planes are symbolized by it, and whenever we visualize upon the star we bring into our subjective consciousness these three worlds, with the mental world rising above them. Suppose we were to reverse the star, as in fact is sometimes done. In the practice of the Black Art, the Pentagram is often reversed. This will mean not Manas rising above the four lower principles, dominating them, standing as the Crown of Glory over the four principles, but sinking below them, crushed down by the weight of the lower principles, being submerged. It will mean Mind conquered by the desire, the body, etc., therefore, if employed in this way, it is for the purpose of crushing the mind of a victim under the weight of desire and physical sensation. It would be employed for the definite purpose of causing one to go insane.

The idea symbolized by the star with the point directly overhead, is the development of Manas as the crown of all the lower principles, and thus ascending toward Buddhi. It is thus the symbol of man, in fact Manas means Man as well as Mind. The idea of Manas and Mind as being identical has grown quite popular among a great many people. It has been assumed that because Manas represented Man, in fact that the word means Man, that none but men had minds. But the thought really presented there is that Manas is the human keynote. Other animals have other keynotes and man has this Manasic principle as his keynote, at the present stage of development. The race is mental in contradistinction to other races of beings, that is to different orders of animals, plants, etc. The higher principles have not yet come into evidence in the case of practically all of the human race. Because Manas is the keynote of Man and is the highest principle that has come into any degree of prominence, man is spoken of as being mind. However, the next step in evolution is Buddhi. Manas should really rise up until it is united with Buddhi. This is the true course of human evolution and as the star is drawn in this way, with the fifth principle, Manas reaching up, striving to unite with the sixth, or Buddhi, which is represented by that just above the star, above Manas, it symbolizes this idea— Manas striving for Buddhi, thus indicating the direction of education and of evolution.

Another thought brought out by the symbol is the Mental Body reaching up and striving to unite with the Mental Plane; the microcosmic Manas, striving after union with the macrocosmic Manas. When this union is accomplished one becomes the Mahatma, the great soul, or great spirit, the great Mind. It is this that is alluded to by the Platonists and other philosophers;—the Greeks when they eulogized the Nous. The Nous is the Mind and when we see how wonderfully it is praised, how it is lauded to the skies by the philosophers, we can see very clearly that they are not thinking of the ordinary mind; it is something much greater than that. As a matter of fact, it is the individual Nous merged in the Kosmic Nous, so that they become one. This state of

THE PENTAGRAM

union is one of the suggestions made by the Pentagram. Another thing suggested by it is that as it points upward, mind is ever rising from the lower to the higher thoughts; the trend of mental culture should be from the concrete to the absolute. We should rise from the Mental to the Causal Body by abstract thought. Philosophy should go into abstraction. When we realize this, we see that modern education is a process of reversing the points of the Star. It is really Black Art that is being practiced by the modern scientist for the tendency of modern thought is to go from the abstract to the concrete. In this way the point is drawn down. We cease to reach after that which is above, but go to that which is below. Mind is brought down in conjunction with the body, with the lower principles. Mind is valued only as a means of acquiring knowledge in regard to the material world, in regard to the physical. Philosophy no longer studies in the transcendental region, but merely in the physical. It consists of the concrete, the phenomenal world. Thus we see the complete reversal of the true purpose of the mind. It is brought into bondage to the appearance of things and even to the material, whereas, its true office is to rise above matter, above desire, and lead one on, through abstract thought until he is able to reach Buddhi where he will be able to cognize the thing in itself and thus escape the illusions of time and space.

The Pentagram teaches us that the true purpose of mind is to pass from the relative to the absolute and to study the relative in relation to the absolute. In other words Manas should look to Buddhi for its guidance, for its inspiration. It should be employed deductively rather than inductively. One should know with the pure reason of Buddhi, should realize the fundamental universal principles and then these principles should be applied to the phenomenal world. Thus mind should be employed in the light of the pure reason or Buddhi. In this way we will be able to deal with the relative in the light of the absolute instead of bringing the absolute in bondage to the relative. Instead of trying to deal with abstractions in the terms of the concrete, we will deal with the concrete in the terms of the abstract. The point ever reaching upward, indicating that the base of all our thinking

OCCULT GEOMETRY

must be beyond thought, it is not in mind, but above and transcending mind that we find the basis for thinking. It is in the light of absolute truth that all thought must be performed. When we learn this lesson, we will cease to study the phenomenal world to find the source of the transcendental world; we will cease to take the phenomenal as the basis by which to try to understand the transcendental world, tracing analogies between the transcendental and the phenomenal worlds, but will accept the transcendental as the foundation and then by our minds, trace analogies between the transcendental and the phenomenal. Thus we will understand the phenomenal world, comparing it with the noumenal world. On the Hermetic principle, "As above, so below," we will know what is above, in the transcendental world and will know that the phenomenal world is but a reflection of this transcendental world, and therefore, is just like it.

The Pentagram teaches us, consequently, that Manas should be the hand maiden of Buddhi; not the one who comes before, but the one who follows after and does the bidding of the mistress.

Another of the suggestions by the Star is this: the five points proceed in five different directions from one common center which is a circle breaking up into five branches. This easily represents five streams of force issuing from one common center of force, a volume sending forth five streams which as they shoot upward, gradually come to a point by reason of the centripetal tendency. What is the suggestion of this? The five points represent Rupa, Linga Sharira, Prana, Kama and Manas, the five lower principles. These are all proceeding from one principle in the center, which is neither of them;—something which is neither Rupa, Linga Sharira, Prana, Kama or Manas, which is neither gross matter, physical ether, prana, desire stuff or mind, but something which contains in itself all those principles undifferentiated, emanating or manifesting these different principles. What principle is that? The Inner Akasha or Buddhi, or Essence of Matter, the ultimate matter, in fact, Kosmic energy the fourth octave. It has been shown in the gross, in motion; but remember that from the Inner Akasha emanates manas, kama, together with prana and the true Akasha

THE PENTAGRAM

or physical ether, in fact the ultimate atoms of these three octaves are Kosmos formed by the uniting of a number of Buddhic atoms; therefore, these three primates are but three manifestations of the Inner Akasha by reason of the lower—of the vibration to the three separate octaves below, therefore, all these principles are emanating from the one principle, Buddhi. The star perfectly represents this, showing the five streams proceeding from the one center, Buddhi. This is true of the different bodies in man as well as of the corresponding principles in the universe. The Pentagram in pointing upward to Buddhi, really teaches the lesson of the fivefold differentiation returning to its source, returning unto and uniting with that from which it sprang, in other words, all those principles working in harmony with Buddhi and the mind fully recognizing this truth, fully becoming conscious of it.

The Pentagram is the particular emblem of the Freemasons, and as such, teaches us that the real secret of Masonry is the recognition of this truth, the septenary nature of man and the universe and the harmony and unity of the manifested or phenomenal with the noumenal or transcendental. The real work of Masonry is to find this, to leave the phenomenal and reach the transcendental, to find the thing in itself and from this construct a philosophy of the eternal world, a philosophy which will teach the nature of the external by its analogy to the internal instead of teaching it merely phenomenally by the study of appearance and even trying to develop the spiritual from the material. This system of philosophy is the structure which Masons are trying to build, they as Free and Accepted Masons should build this structure, this "House not made with hands, eternal in the heavens," which will be realized when they have accomplished this philosophical structure; that is to say, this structure which they are building, the interpretation of the materials in the terms of the transcendental, will accomplish the conquest of the material world, the acquisition of all material knowledge and thus, will prepare the way for the building of God. The Master Mason is one who has risen above the mind and is able to function on the Buddhic Plane of Consciousness.

OCCULT GEOMETRY

Another suggestion is this: the race has developed Manas. The next step in the evolution will be Buddhi. The Coming Race must develop Buddhi in conjunction with Manas. The star ever points upward, signifying that the future trend must be toward Buddhi, that the education necessary for the information of the race is one passing from Manas to Buddhi.

Again, the star which in its center represents Buddhi and its upper part Manas in the individual, points to the Buddhi above, indicating that it is by the union of the individual Buddhi with the Universal Buddhi, or Buddhic Plane, that the Light for the Coming Race is to come, also indicating that it must come through one who has solved the Mystery of the Pentagram and has become united with the Kosmic Buddhi, thus indicating that a Buddha must come and open the way, must be the channel through which the individual mind may be raised to Buddhi and thus the Buddhic Race be made possible. The Star thus signifies both the universal Manas and the individual Manas and teaches the Mystery of Initiation on the Mental and Buddhic Planes, and has been used from time immemorial to symbolize this idea.

LESSON VIII

THE HEXAGRAM

The HEXAGRAM—the Seal of Solomon—is made by interlacing two triangles, one pointing forward and the other pointing in such a way as to form a six-pointed star.

This has in all ages been one of the most sacred of geometric symbols, representing a number of things; first, in regard to the human soul, it symbolizes Buddhi, the sixth principle, beginning at the bottom going upward. Just as the Pentagram symbolizes Manas, the fifth principle, pointing forward to Buddhi, the Hexagram represents Manas after it has been lost in Buddhi. Just as the Pentagram is the symbol of man as he is, the Hexagram symbolizes the man of the future, who will have six distinct principles functioning in his outer (or true) consciousness. The psychic, physical threshold will at that time have been pushed back so as to leave Buddhi on this side of the threshold. As it is now this threshold intervenes between Manas and Buddhi, leaving both Buddhi and Atma beyond the threshold. In the man of the future this threshold will be pushed back so that Atma alone will be beyond. Buddhi will thus represent the highest attainment of man's outer consciousness.

Another meaning of the Hexagram is that of the spiritual and material trinities, the triangle always representing a trinity. Trinity, as you will remember, is the symbol of Divinity in unity, being the separation of the one force into two principles, electricity and magnetism and the converging of these two principles at a given point; in other words, the Law of Opposites and the Law of Balance working in harmony. It is thus the separation into the two principles,

OCCULT GEOMETRY

positive and negative, and then the bringing together into the united principles, that future manifestation may be made possible.

The figure is usually drawn with one triangle WHITE and the other BLACK, signifying the spiritual and material. These two trinities are interlaced, so that all life is the outgrowth of harmonious activity of spiritual and material principles, each acting upon the other. Spirit thus raises matter and matter draws down spirit. The universe has not become entirely materialized, neither entirely spiritualized. It is the process of the Spirit's descent into matter continually going on.

In the human constitution the spiritual trinity, or triangle, represents, Atma, Buddhi, Manas. The material trinity Rupa, Prana, Linga Sharira, being the material principles of same grade. You will notice that Kama the desire principle, is not included. It is in fact the line which differentiates the two. Thus we see Desire expressing itself in two directions; the forward triangle is ever leading Desire forward through Mind, Soul and Spirit, while the lower triangle is life and ether into gross physical sensation.

We may say, therefore, that the direction of the triangle indicates whether desire is acting under physical sensation, or under the higher spiritual gratification. The desire nature is the parting of the ways. Man must express himself according to the nature of his desires, and as is the desire activity in its direction, so will be the course of man's development.

Again we may look at the Hexagram as representing the united body, and then we will get another view of the symbol. The lower triangle will represent the physical body, the magnetic body and the desire body. The upper triangle the Spirit, the Soul and the Causal Body, making the median line pass through the mental body. Thus we will see concrete thought as the parting of the way, between the material and spiritual triangles.

If one allows his thoughts to dwell on material things, on the expression of modern nonsense denominated Physical Science, he will be degraded to the level of the animals; he will be ever drawn downward into the material, his whole

THE HEXAGRAM

being becoming merged into matter. The whole trend of physical research is consequently toward materialism. On the other hand, he may turn his thought to philosophy and metaphysics, and by investigating in this way, his mind will be lifted up so that he will function in the higher trinity. Man, as we see him, is always represented by the interlacing of these triangles. We do not see one as wholly spiritual, in the sense of the upper triangle, or wholly material in the sense of the lower triangle. He represents the two triangles in a state of interlacement.

If you will notice the two figures carefully, the Hexagram is an improvement over the diamond. The diamond represents the two triangles with their lines together, the base of the upper triangle resting squarely on the top line of the lower one, while the Hexagram represents this lower triangle slipped up half way on the upper one, interlacing the same.

Now, if we continue slipping it up it will ultimately reach a point where the upper line of the lower triangle will exactly touch the base line of the upper triangle. In this way we will have a figure representing in the center a diamond with two "X's," so to speak, on either side, forming a diamond. You will see in this way, how they are becoming separated.

Now, a half circle must be described which will bring the two triangles into a state of absolute coincidence, thus being slid up into the spiritual, the spiritual descending into the material, in the sense of taking its place, and this state will represent the drawing up of the lower principles.

Now, we have in the Nirvani, one who has drawn his physical principles up into the emotional or astral, and the Para-Nirvani, one whose astral nature has been drawn up into the mental. Thus the Para-Nirvani represents the one who has solved the problem of the Pentagram.

Were one to feel so that spirit, soul and causal body would entirely disappear so that he were incapable of anything but concrete thought, this would be the outgrowth of his emotional nature.

In one ruled absolutely by his physical sensations and so incapable of acting differently, we would have one who would accomplish the same work, only the spiritual triangle would

OCCULT GEOMETRY

have been swallowed up in the material instead of the material in the spiritual. Thus is represented the two great problems which the soul confronts.

We must also understand another aspect of the Hexagram, namely, the macrocosm and the microcosm. In this, one is the Kosmic triangle, the other the Individual triangle. We see thus that man has been partially individual and partially under the sway of the Kosmic. In his constitution the two forces are interlaced. His entire being represents an interplaying of the two forces, Kosmos and Individuality. We see in the lesson on the diamond, that these two are usually in absolute opposition.

We see in the type of the man of the future, and, to a certain extent in the highest type of the man of the present, the interlacing of the two forces, the recognition of the Kosmic world—to a certain extent Kosmic Consciousness, finding this great Kosmic force working in and through all life.

But as yet there is a certain amount of controversy between the individual and the Kosmos. It is possible in time, however, for the revolution to take place which causes the individual triangle to exactly coincide with the Kosmic. In this way we become no longer individuals. Our individuality is lost, we become merely instruments in the hands of the Kosmos, absolutely passive under its control, and in this state of passivity, what do we do? We embody the fullness of the Kosmos. Having renounced individuality, we individualize all things, learn all lessons of life and live them.

Another lesson taught by the Hexagram is indicated by the inside. You will notice that the interior of the Hexagram is composed of six equal surfaces where all the lines cross these six equal surfaces forming a hexagonal figure which represents the result of the interlacing of the two triangles.

The individual who has accomplished this work of interlacement, presents the picture of one having six principles in full manifestation instead of five. In other words, an Adept, a Master of Wisdom, and why is this?

To recognize the individual and kosmic trinities is to recognize the unreality of individual existence and realize that the individual is merely an expression of the universal; that he merely indicates an expression, a channel through

THE HEXAGRAM

which the Kosmos manifests. This means Kosmic Consciousness.

One who has solved the lesson of the Hexagram has, therefore, overcome the illusion of personality, and has recognized the Kosmic relation; has overcome, also, the illusion of time and space and sees that all things are manifestations of a trinity. When he discovers that the individual is always an expression of the universal and that there is always a spiritual and a material trinity, he has learned better than to accept the scientific dogma that man has evolved from the lowest forms and that all activity is merely the expression of materiality, recognizing the inter-relation of matter and spirit. Such a person can never be deceived by the dogmas of so-called science. He has passed through the realm of thought, mind and intellect to that of reason and intuitive intelligence. Thus the Buddha is the result of the recognition of the mystery of the Hexagram. As it represents all individuals in connection with the universe, and the interlacing of spirit and matter in all those individuals, the solving of its problem must necessarily make one master of spirit and matter.

It also teaches us the eternal war between spirit and matter, that is the struggle for supremacy, as was taught by Zarathushtra and all the other sages of the past, this war is raging in two opposite directions. If spirit gains the ascendency then matter will be drawn up into spirit, in other words, spiritualized, completely dominated by spirit. The three planes, or rather principles of matter, will then be only vehicles for the expression of the principles of spirit.

On the other hand, if matter gains the ascendency over spirit, spirit will be drawn down into matter, be swallowed up, in other words, the three principles of spirit will be completely engulfed in the three principles of matter, becoming merely vehicles of expression in a certain sense completely partaking of the nature of matter.

The eternal is consequently vibrating at all times between these two forces. Neither one seems to gain the ascendency. There is a balance between the two forces which at all times preserves the equilibrium. The one who is between the two, that is who has them perfectly balanced in his being, is thus a master of both triangles, master in the realm of spirit and

OCCULT GEOMETRY

master in the realm of matter, and likewise knows both, and is the Aseka Adept, the Perfect Master, the Perfect Man.

The Hexagram signifies for us, in this sense, the Aseka Adept, whereas, the Pentagram signifies the ordinary man. As the Pentagram is the measure of a man, so is the Hexagram the measure of the Aseka Adept, the Perfect Man.

We can now understand why the Hexagram was employed as the Seal of King Solomon, the Perfect Master of Wisdom.

LESSON IX

THE SEVEN-POINTED STAR

The SEVEN-POINTED STAR is a star formed with seven points radiating equal distances. It is really a center sending forth seven currents of force and hence signifies the seven principles coming from one common center. The spirit sends forth its own ray and six modified rays. Thus we have here the idea of Spirit manifesting all the principles of the Universe.

Another suggestion is that of something beyond the Spirit, namely, the Divine Spirit sending forth the seven rays of nature, the seven manifestations of the Universe.

Again we have suggested the thought of each plane of nature sending forth seven rays or seven notes of the octave, each of a different order.

We have again the suggestion of the seven prismatic rays of the seven colors of the spectrum, being the sevenfold manifestation of one force, one principle.

Further, we have in the human being the seven principles which are the sevenfold manifestation of the entity.

Further, we may by this seven-pointed star represent the descent of the Fohatic Force into its diverse manifestations. In this Fohatic Force we must realize first the idea of boundless space as the substance of all things; second, infinite force applied to boundless space, acting upon or generating the diverse activities. From this thought flows forth the idea of the seven rays expressing themselves in the seven properties of matter, such as sound, color, form and the others, so that we have the seven activities of energy acting upon force. These seven activities thus give expression to these seven forms of material activity, which express themselves through

OCCULT GEOMETRY

the seven principles; thus we have the forty-nine forces growing out of the sevenfold activity of Fohat. The Universe is conceived to be the product of these forty-nine forces. Thus the seven-pointed star becomes the symbol of the Spirit's descent into matter.

Another conception of it, is in the modification of the Great Breath, the Great Breath being conceived of as this force, of which Atma, Buddhi, Manas, Kama, Prana, Linga Sharira and the physical universe are the seven modifications. We have here the Great Breath acting upon these seven principles on the five planes of nature,—expressing itself on all those planes, giving expression to the five or seven Tattvas, as the case may be on each of those planes, acting upon each principle.

Another form in which this septenary idea is presented is in the solid septenary figure, that is a figure with seven sides. This figure, if you will observe closely, is practically the same as the seven-pointed star only with the rays reversed. The points are all together and as they radiate, each being cut off squarely will represent a figure with seven sides, that is, assuming a flat surface. If you assume a solid, resembling a cube, in a certain sense you will find there will still be seven equal surfaces. Now, the difference between the star and this septenary figure is the presentation of a circle in the star, symbolizing unity, from which the various points converge. It does not, therefore, represent any particular activity but rather the sevenfold rays of the center or the circle of infinity. On the other hand, if you conceive of the septenary figure the rays are passing out from a point rather than a circle, indicating the beginning; not the idea of unity, but the starting point, and the rays as they come forth, broaden, presenting a flat surface, thus this figure represents the manifestation of the seven principles. It is purely a symbol of manifestation, whereas, the seven-pointed star is a symbol rather of the septenary diversity and unity without any thought of manifestation.

Another figure of great value in the study of any geometry, is the Circle with a point in its center. Inasmuch as the circle alone is the symbol of unity, we have here the point of manifestation, the point at which manifestation begins, the

THE SEVEN-POINTED STAR

starting point of activity where force begins, when the first outward or manifesting, pushing impulse is imparted, followed by a continual extending of the circle of unity. This circle of unity indicates that all the manifestation is one; that it is Kosmos, that the universe is not dualistic, but monistic, that all manifestation, no matter how far it may go, still preserves substantial unity with that from which it started. The Universe being an expansion of God's first idea, being objectification of that idea and that idea being the natural outgrowth of the Divine, is such an idea as only the Divine can produce, hence the universe partakes of the substantial nature of its Divine Architect. Therefore, we are not to recognize physical causation, natural law or anything of the kind, but are to recognize in the universe the manifestation of God. For this reason a careful understanding of the unity of God is essential and a proper understanding of nature. Nature must not be studied in departments by specialization, but by generalization. We must study it as a Kosmos, not as a member of fragmentary pieces.

Still another symbol represents a circle divided by a horizontal line into upper and lower departments. The meaning of this is the complete equilibrium of all the activities of the universe—between the electric and magnetic principles. All unity is the product of that activity; the perfect equilibrium is continually maintained. There is never any deviation from this principle. In no department of Nature will we find absence of this differentiation. It may be latent, but it is still there. All force, all activity, all life are the products of the twofold activity of electric and magnetic force on all the planes of nature. Where two lines cross, forming a cross any place within a circle, we are to recognize the meaning as being practically the same as that of the Swastika—the wheel, the Cross of Fire revolving in space, only the Swastika offers the suggestion of a sentinel, the sentinel being always the symbol of matter, while the circle is the symbol of unity. This represents, therefore, the unity of the Kosmos as the result of harmonious activity of the positive and negative, electric and magnetic forces. Thus all the universe is operative on that fourfold differentiation; therefore, we see the cross enclosed within a circle as the symbol of that perfect unity growing out of the differentiation of the two principles. When the Cross stands alone, the crossing in the middle of the circle removed, it indicates lack of unity—that is, that unity has not been realized. The activity is going on, but no particular effect of such manifestation has as yet come into being.

When the Cross is reversed, that is the top piece at the bottom, we have the idea not of the one force dividing into the electric and magnetic, but rather of the electric and magnetic forces coming together, uniting and forming the conjunction of the two, as the drawing in of the manifested into the unmanifested.

Another important symbol which is also electrical in its character, is the Lamb Skin, or White Apron, of the Freemason. This White Apron is in two pieces, so to speak, a square and a triangle, with the triangle in the apron descending into the square. The septenary principle is thus indicated by the square and the triangle; the square indicating the lower four principles, that is the lower four notes of any octave, and the triangle indicating the higher three principles or rather the three higher notes of the octave. Thus the trinity of the undifferentiated principle and its electric and magnetic differentiation is represented by the triangle, while the square indicates the four lower notes of positive and negative—electricity and magnetism. Also by the square is indicated the two physical principles, or life principle, and kama or desire and will. Atma, Buddhi, Manas are indicated by the triangle. The applicant enters the Lodge wearing his apron with the triangle turned under at the side, thus showing only the square; indicating, therefore, that he is still under the bondage of the Law of Opposites, not having solved it, and also, that he is functioning on the lower planes and has not yet reached mental liberation, the triune of Atma, Buddhi, Manas, has not yet come to him, neither has he recognized the source of manifestation. He is acting exclusively in the relative. When the fellow craftsman realizes it, it will turn up into view, be above the square, thus indicating that at this stage he recognizes the Law of Opposites and knows what it is, but he does not yet realize its relation to the manifested; neither does he recognize the

THE SEVEN-POINTED STAR

relation of the absolute to the relative. The Master allows the triangle to descend into the square, thus indicating the domination of the lower by the higher, of matter by spirit, and that he, having united the trinity of Atma, Buddhi, Manas, is now able to dominate his lower principles. This also indicates the domination of the lower principles of the universe by the higher trinity, and from this we can understand the nature of the problem.

One of the most important lessons in Geometry, is taught in the 47th Problem of Euclid. It is something like this: What is it the perpendicular of which is 3/4 of the base and the base 4/5 of the hypothenuse? This means a figure with the base line represented by 4 a horizontal, the perpendicular by 3, and the hypothenuse line by 5. You will see that these together represent 12 and 12 is the figure that squares the circle. As a matter of fact, this problem is solved in man; it is the measure of a Man. The base line of 4 represents the foundation of the four lower principles, and the upright—three higher principles are in Atma, Buddhi, Manas. Thus we have a septenary represented by the four lower principles as the foundation and the three higher as the structure. Five is the number of man. The hypothenuse being five represents man as combining in himself both the latitude and the base. The hypothenuse as man is consequently both the upper and lower, the square and the triangle, perfectly united. Because five, it is the principle of Manas, the principle of man. Its force has only begun the upward climb; it has reached only Manas, the lowest of the latitude principles, not having reached Buddhi, or Atma. The magnetic body, the astral body, the life principle, are the foundation, the base line while the mental, and causal bodies, taken here as one—and the Buddhic and Atmic principles represent the latitude. These two unite in man, the most perfectly formed body in creation. Man is thus seen to be in deed and in truth the microcosm of the universe because he unites in himself the trinity and the quarternary in a state of balance.

The universe is represented by the perpendicular and the horizontal—the entire fullness of nature—and man, the hypothenuse, embodies all of the universe. It teaches man

OCCULT GEOMETRY

as the microcosm of the macrocosm.

Further, we find that 12 is the sum of the universe and man, representing the two—man and the universe, and as 12 is the squaring of the trinity we have, therefore, in man a note of 3, the symbol of the law of balance, the universe acting in and through man. Thus the two principles that usually divide, the two differentiations, electricity and magnetism, are balanced in the universe always, likewise they are balanced in man, finding in him their perfect expression —the little world is found in man. Thus we find the perfect realization of all things in nature. The hypothenuse or 5 is thus the uniting of the horizontal 4, and the perpendicular 3. It thus gives the measure of man and the measure of the universe. It shows, likewise, the mind is that principle through which all the universe is recognized, both the material and the spiritual. Thus the lesson taught by this problem, the problem which has bothered geometricians,—they do not know it is purely psychological and metaphysical and is to be understood in this way.

When we realize what has been said in regard to the seven-pointed star, the septenary figure, we will understand why seven has been the complete number; why it is the great number, the great septenary; not because of any arbitrary consideration, but due to the fact that it radiates seven rays; that all manifestation is by sevens, that there is no escape from it. Seven has been the great number of the universe and the great number of man and of everything else—of God as well because the starting point, the beginning of manifestation, falls along the septenary path. Unity is manifested in seven directions and thus seven directions were present—a sevenfold unity. For this reason the septenary figure is most properly employed as the sacred symbol of nature, of the universe, of man, of God.

Seven rays divide themselves into seven others, hence seven, the proper figure for each principle in the universe, and so we might take each one of those notes and find that it manifests in seven different principles, and so the septenary division might be carried on ad infinitum. Seven is thus the

THE SEVEN-POINTED STAR

great symbol number because all manifestation is septenary; all creation is septenary; the Universe is a sevenfold unity. It is not, therefore, arbitrary, but is really the exact nature of all things. Seven has ever been employed by the Kaballa as the number of completion.

LESSON X

THE CUBE

The CUBE, as is, of course, well known, is a figure having eight surfaces of equal dimensions and equal form, being in other words, eight square surfaces and a figure containing three dimensions.

The Cube is really two squares, one lifted above the other, with the lines connecting them. We may say, therefore, it symbolizes in the first place the square above and one below, that is, the material and spiritual squares. The square is practically the same as the Swastika in its meaning, representing as it does, the division of electricity and magnetism into the positive and negative poles. Thus we have from one point the flowing out of the four currents, expressing the Square of Manifestation and as the manifesting square on the physical plane becomes the four elements of

Nitrogen — Tangiferous Ether — Touch — Air
Oxygen   — Luminiferous Ether — Sight — Fire
Hydrogen — Gustiferous Ether — Taste — Water
Carbon   — Odoriferous Ether — Smell — Earth

We have thus in the lower square the entire realm of physical matter, all the atoms symbolized as well as the mineral, vegetable and animal kingdoms, everything in fact, on the physical plane as the manifestation of the trinity. Again it must be borne in mind that these four ethers are merely the result of the differentiation of electricity and magnetism into the positive and negative forces. Therefore, we have electricity and magnetism as being also contained and as these are but the twofold differentiation of the undifferentiated ether, we may say that the manifestation of the ultimate physical atom into the diverse physical forces

THE CUBE

and forms of matter—into everything, in fact, of a physical character, is symbolized by the lower square.

The upper square is that of the Spirit and so the tangiferous ether, the luminiferous ether, the gustiferous ether and the odoriferous ether are the fourfold manifestations on the Spiritual plane. All the other activities of the Spirit, everything on the Spiritual plane is a manifestation of an organization growing out of the union and combination of the atoms of these four elements—these ethers. Therefore, the entire spiritual plane or realm of the universal spirit, is but the expression of these four principles which are spiritual electricity and magnetism, both positive and negative, polarized.

The square is again a positive and negative polarization of spiritual electricity and magnetism, these being in turn, the masculine and feminine aspects of the highest or undifferentiated spirit above. Thus we have the tangiferous ether on both the physical and spiritual planes, manifesting in the form of luminiferous ether, gustiferous ether, and odoriferous ether, which in turn manifest all the universe.

We have then in the Cube, the manifestation symbolically expressed, of the spiritual and physical planes of the universe from one central point.

Now, it will be noticed that in order to form the Cube there must be four lines standing as corner posts, so to speak, from the upper, the spiritual, down to the lower, the physical. These symbolize the fourfold differentiation, the square of the intervening planes of nature, indicating that the astral and mental as well as the Buddhic planes, are susceptible to this same fourfold differentiation, being the upper trinity differentiated into the lower quarternary or square. It is a case of the square and triangle all the way through. But we are not to understand that the trinity stands absolutely alone as it were, for the trinity itself is the beginning of the square, each of the principles, that is the electric and magnetic, merely dividing so as to manifest in two different directions. Thus we see the fourfold division in the twofold present in the trinity. Therefore, it is really the one principle being squared, as in one sense, the trinity represents the circle, the circle being always equivalent to number

OCCULT GEOMETRY

one, being, as it is, the electrical symbol of unity.

Again in three, the triangle, we have the symbol of unity—diversity reduced to unity, practically the same as the circle.

Now, in the square as the manifestation, we have the problem of squaring the circle—life on all planes of Nature. The lower square represents squaring of the circle on the physical plane and that is, in fact, the very key to the manifestation. Also the physical plane gives us a case of the squaring of the circle—likewise the intervening three planes. Thus we might say the Cube symbolizes Nature, the Kosmos, as the circle squared, that is, shows the Kosmos as the manifestation of the ultimate first principle on all the different planes. It shows that the undifferentiated principle before manifestation has begun, is the beginning of all things, in the essence of the Kosmos.

In another sense it may be used to symbolize the unmanifested God. It is not often so used, but it may be used, properly, as such, showing that manifestation is contained in the unmanifest potentially and merely to flow out into expression.

In the psychical sense the Cube means one who has mastered these things, one who has mastered the five planes of Nature and has thoroughly harmonized the manifest with the unmanifest, reducing them to a state of absolute unity; the master on all the planes of nature, the Aseka Adept—the Perfect Man; the Jivan-Mukta, who has become a Free Spirit without having lost mastery on any of the lower planes. Such a one is represented by the Cube, being equal in every direction complete on the spiritual and physical planes and on all the intervening planes; one in whom each principle has been perfected and remains absolutely perfected on the plane of nature to which it belongs. Such is the meaning of the Cube when applied as the MEASURE OF A MAN.

Again, the Cube is used very appropriately to symbolize Para-Nirvana in the sense that the seven principles in man are included in the septenary, the eighth representing something above man—an eighth principle added. Thus when man has attained Para-Nirvana, that is when his individual spirit has been completely merged in the universal spirit the individuality has disappeared and the individual is com-

THE CUBE

pletely merged in the universal; having lost all individual identity, he has passed from the realm of Ishvara to the realm of Brahman. The distinction between the two is this: Brahman represents the universal Atman, the Spirit undifferentiated, that which is still, that which has not descended into manifestation, the unmanifest spirit; that which has not yet become manifest, and as we grasp this thought we see then in this the spirit of absolute unity with no variation, with no attribute, but containing all attributes in a state of latency, not in a state of manifestation; that is to say, it is capable of all attributes but actually has none. When we realize this we will be prepared to see the distinction, for Ishvara represents the aspect of the universal spirit which is manifested, which has crystallized into different forms, reproducing different spirits. All the spirits in the universe, all the concrete spirits collectively constitute Ishvara. The abstract spirit before it has taken concrete form, before it has manifested as a spirit, being, therefore, a simple spirit, as Brahman. One is always on the plane of Ishvara, that is, his spirit is a part of Ishvara. The Nirvani is one whose spirit has been brought to the highest state of perfection, who is thus a part of Ishvara, having an individual spirit developed to the highest point to which it may develop and still retain its individuality. This is the state of Nirvana, but when one reaches Para-Nirvana, his individual spirit has been merged in the universal spirit. He loses all identity, all differentiation, having embodied the fullness or completeness of undifferentiated universal spirit; he has thus passed the line "Pass not," that is, the line which the individual cannot pass. In order to pass this line he must leave his individuality behind.

It has been said by the Oriental teachers that no one can retain his astral principle and attain Para-Nirvana; he must leave that completely behind. In attaining Nirvana it is necessary to leave the body behind. This merely means that one renounces his own feelings, his own emotions—must become absolutely emotionless before he can attain that state for he has left individuality behind. Thus his emotional principle, his desire body is drawn up into the mental, individual desires having disappeared, he is thus swallowed up into the higher principles. The seven lower principles all of which are built upon the principle of individuality, are now swallowed up by that which is devoid of all individuality, into the realm of abstract spirit—Para-Nirvana. Thus the seven principles of man have been swallowed up by that which is to man, the eighth principle because it is not in him,—that is the state of abstract spirit. This state of abstract spirit swallows up the seven individual or concrete principles of man, takes their places and becomes the keynote of his being. Nevertheless, the eighth is all the seven principles of Nature because the universal spirit is the first principal of Nature, or the seventh if you begin from the physical and go upward. The seventh principle of the Kosmos is the source of all the spirits of the universe. Thus, that which is the eighth principle of man is the seventh of the universe, Ishvara the concrete spirit, and the abstract spirit or Brahman, being really two aspects of one and the same thing. Thus although the man has left manifestation behind, he is still on the seventh principle of Nature. It is the eighth principle of man, but the seventh of the universe. Thus the eighth is of the seventh and this is what the Cube means when applied to man.

The Cube, when taken Kosmically, teaches that this is the process of the universe. The general tendency of all things is for the manifested universe to be drawn back into the spirit. It is that disintegrating principle—that principle which ever lives by reason of the process of perpetual change. This ever-changing process is what the Hindus mean by the universe going into Pralaya. It is the continual tendency of the manifest to return to the unmanifest. It is the ebb and flow of all things. It shows that the manifested universe is but the Manvantara of the abstract spirit and it inevitably draws the universe back—that is the manifested back into its abstract—its Pralaya. But it must not be understood that there are definite periods of Pralaya Manvantara. This is an error. The meaning is that the atoms composing the universe are continually going through this change. The universe is always and so is the realm of the abstract spirit, but there is continual change. Some of the atoms are going into pralaya, others going forth into manvantara; this process

THE CUBE

of change is continually going on. Thus we have the seven principles of the manifested universe as the emanations—the liberations of the unmanifested abstract spirit and we see them again returning to this spirit, although this spirit is a part of the first principle of the Kosmos and, therefore, is included in the seven.

The tendency of all things to enter Para-Nirvana is thus taught by the Cube; likewise, Para-Nirvana as the destiny of the souls of all things if they go on far enough—as the goal of human evolution, just as it is the goal of the universe to ultimately become the perfect manifestation of the abstract.

We see, therefore, the Cube as the symbol of the perfected universe, as well as of perfercted man. Here we have another argument for the truth that man is the microcosm of the universe. The perfect man is represented by the Cube, likewise, the perfect universe. The little Cube is the Para-Nirvana; the big Cube, the great Cube is the Perfected Universe, the universe having manifested Para-Nirvana. It is to symbolize these truths that the Cube is employed and whereever employed in geometrical symbolism it means the same.

The Cube when used with reference to the Kosmos reveals the tendency to return to the Spirit. It is, in other words, a symbol of the Spirit's descent into matter and of the return of the universe to Spirit, symbolizing the Great Return. The same is true in regard to Man.

LESSON XI

THE SPHERE

The SPHERE is formed by the union of three circles in such a way as to present six semi-circular lines forming a suggestion of a sphere. Of course, it may be filled in by a number of other lines. We might, for instance, have twenty-one circles which would make it much more closed, but it is intended to represent three circles, each within the other in such a way as to form the Sphere.

The Circle, while symbolizing unity, also presents the idea of trinity, in fact the Sphere presents in the three circles three trinities.

Again, if we take the Circle here as the symbol of unity we would have nine circles and what they really symbolize is unity including three trinities; therefore, it is the geometrical symbol of nine being the mathematical number. It represents the world and is the symbol of the world. It is to be understood as a world including three trinities, therefore, nine distinct numbers. We have, then the ninth principle including all the others, as the significance of the Sphere. It, therefore, is the symbol of Maha-Para-Nirvana. Now what is Maha-Para-Nirvana? We learn in the lesson on the Cube that Para-Nirvana is that state in which the individual spirit has been swallowed up in the universal spirit; has merged itself in that spirit, becoming one with it, at the same time having drawn up the desire nature into the Mind so that it had disappeared, as an individual principle. But the main thing to be noticed here is that a Para-Nirvani is one whose individual spirit has been united with and completely merged into the universal spirit, the undifferentiated spirit, which is, however, the manifesting God. Just as the

THE SPHERE

Ishvara, or the Nirvanic plane, is the Spirit individualized, including all the individual spirits collectively, likewise, Para-Nirvana is the universal spirit before individualization has taken place. Now, as we lose sight of individualization and completely merge the individuality into that which has no individuality, thus losing all individuality and uniting the individual spirit or entity with that universal spirit, so that it ceases to be an entity and becomes merely a channel through which the universal spirit flows, responding to all its emotions and partaking absolutely, we have the full realization of Para-Nirvana. Now Maha-Para-Nirvana, or the ninth principle is the Divine Spirit, the unmanifest God, Para-Brahman, and when we have completely merged our being, our spirit in the Divine Spirit, so that the union has taken place, the human spirit is lost in the Divine, and therefore, hears and responds to impulses coming from the universal spirit and only to those proceeding from the Divine Spirit, being positive to the Universal Spirit, negative to the Divine Spirit, and therefore, responds only to the impulses of the latter,—we have now passed from the eighth to the ninth principle—from Brahman to Para-Brahman and are now in a state of absolute Divine Unity, and so mind is drawn up into Buddhi, the fifth principle is drawn up into the sixth. We, therefore, have the sixth, seventh, eighth and ninth, in one sense, but as the individual spirit has been merged in the Divine, we may, therefore, say that in the highest sense but two principles left, and that we have left the lower realms and entered this Divine state. The Divine Spirit is now functioning in and through our entity, but there is no ego, in the sense that man has an ego at the time he reaches Para-Nirvana, for it is God, the Divine Spirit, Para-Brahman, that is functioning in and through the entire being. This being the case, man leaves the realm of nature, as it were completely, leaves the natural and is swallowed up in the Divine.

We may say the three circles represented here are the physical circle, consisting of the physical matter, that is the physical body; the magnetic body and the life force, Prana; the mental circle, or the psychical circle, consisting of the Desire Body, Manas and Buddi, and the spiritual circle consisting of the Individual Spirit, the Universal Spirit and the Divine Spirit. Thus we see the perfect illustration, the perfect presentation, as it were, of the condition of the Maha-Para-Nirvana, and the Sphere gives to us a world. We are to see in such a man the little world which is not only the microcosm of the universe, but a microcosm of the Divine Spirit as well—and this is the difference between the Maha-Para-Nirvani and the ordinary Nirvani, or Aseka Adept. The latter is the microcosm of nature, individualization of nature, while the Maha-Para-Nirvani is likewise the microcosm of the Divine Spirit including in him both the natural world and the Divine. Thus we have in man a world including both nature and God. This is the conception of the Maha-Para-Nirvani symbolized by the Sphere when applied to an individual. When applied to the universe it represents practically the same thing, that is the seven principles of the manifested universe, universal spirit as the eighth principle and the Divine Spirit as the ninth.

Now, by this symbol we are to understand that the Divine Spirit is quite as much a part of the universe as is Nature. The universe is not to be conceived of as separate and apart from God, but as being perfectly united with Him. This does not mean, however, that God cannot exist separate from Nature, which is not Pantheism, but absolute Monotheism. The universe co-exists with God and is dependent upon Him; in fact, God is the ninth principle of the universe, or, from the other points of view, the First Principle. The Divine Spirit stands above and is the beginning of the universe. We are not to conceive of creation or existence in any sense as being independent of Divine Spirit, but rather as being of the instigation or emanation of Divine Spirit. In other words, all creation has been by reason of the differentiation of the Divine Spirit; in this way all things have been created, and in no other way.

We are then to understand the universe as being an emanation from God, thus it is not separate, it is the body of God. As the soul may exist without the body, but the body cannot live without the soul, likewise God could exist without the universe, but the universe, or Nature, rather, could not exist without God.

THE SPHERE

The ninth principle, the Divine Spirit is substance, but all the other eight principles are existence, being the mere externalization of the substance—Divine Spirit.

Again, when we take into consideration the return—and this is undoubtedly symbolized by the Sphere, as well as the outflowing or emanation, we are to understand that the universe in its evolution must sooner or later reach a stage of absolute harmony, absolute unity with the Divine Spirit —then must be absolutely swallowed up, united. Thus the universe will be absorbed into the Divine Spirit. This is what is meant by the Maha-Pralaya, the night of Para-Brahman, when all things return to it. This does not, however, mean in the highest sense of its usage, the obliteration of the manifested universe, it rather means the perfection of the universe so that it will be so developed as to give expression to the Divine Spirit. It will become, in other words, a fit vehicle for the expression of that Divine Spirit, so that the phenomenal will entirely disappear and things will seem as they really are. Evolution must produce that state where the beings living upon the earth will perfectly realize the fullness of Divine Spirit, where the Divine will reign supreme over all life. When that state has been reached then, indeed will the Divine Spirit be the ninth principle as well as the first. This means that the world must go through these different stages of progress until the Divine Spirit has become its keynote, the dominating principle of its being. Thus the sphere represents the world with the Divine Spirit as its first principle, its source, likewise, as the ultimate realization of its progress.

We must guard against drifting into the thought of Pantheism. The Pantheistic doctrine absorbs God into the universe, thus denying an extra mundane God. It regards God as merely one principle of the universe, having no existence outside of it, or, we might say, God is a certain spirit in matter quite as dependent upon matter as matter is upon it. In fact the fundamental principle of Pantheism is matter with God as the spirit animating it, dependent upon it to a certain extent. The Pantheist denies God excepting as a certain aspect of the universe, but this conception, as revealed to us by the Sphere, is absolutely Monotheistic. It

OCCULT GEOMETRY

denies the universe; it affirms God as the one principle, the all in all, and the universe as the mere form of manifestation which the Divine Spirit has taken. Thus it is an organism thrown over the spirit, having no real existence, being merely an exemplification of the spirit, also showing the power, Divine Spirit—the substance back of the universe—existence. It is a state which we may reach, a condition of absolute emancipation from nature and natural law. Thus we may say that Maha-Para-Nirvana is a state of spiritual existence transcending nature. Thus we have not only an intra-mundane, but likewise an extra-mundane God. We are, therefore, not Pantheistic but Monotheistic, recognizing not a Spirit which has been absorbed by the universe, but a Spirit which is self-existent—the universe as existence, the spirit as substance. The universal spirit is merely one form or existence of this substance, Divine Spirit.

The Sphere, wherever employed, and whenever employed, symbolizes this aspect of the world, if it is used in reference to the universe. If used in reference to man it symbolizes this particular aspect of man, of the soul. It is not God absorbed in the universe, but the universe emanating from God, the Divine Spirit maintaining its integrity intact after the universe has emanated. In other words, the emanation of the universe does not lessen the Divine Spirit, it still remains transcendent.

Again, we find that every part of the surface of the Sphere is equidistant from its center. Here is a center radiating energy in every direction, thus forming the different aspects of the Sphere and collectively forming the completed Sphere which is really the radiation of energy from a common point, this energy being crystallized to form a solid. This gives us the perfect completion of a universe formed by emanation. It should also teach us this; inasmuch as the surface of the Sphere represents the nine principles including the Divine Spirit, and this surface is the emanation or radiation from a common center, there is something back of the Divine Spirit. It is not the ultimate, but there is a tenth principle, which is in the center of the Sphere, namely Jehovah, standing back of the Divine Spirit and thus emanating the Divine Spirit which, in turn, produces the diverse activities and forces of

THE SPHERE

the universe. Thus we have a Divine Spirit which is the substance of the existent universe called Nature, and this Divine Spirit is, in turn, the existence of a Divine Being who antedates its manifestation. This is what is taught me by the Sphere, namely, the universe including the Divine Spirit, the entire nine principles were an emanation from the Divine Being, Jehovah, the manas of God in all things as the constitution of the universe, but His manas as the radiation of a concealed Unseen God in the hidden center, from whom radiate all things both spiritual and material, both natural and divine. The transcendent spirit, as well as all nature, are thus seen to be mere externalization, emanations, existences of the substance, the transcendent, divine being JEHOVAH.

It is to symbolize this that the SPHERE is employed.

LESSON XII

SQUARING THE CIRCLE

The problem of SQUARING THE CIRCLE, its possibility has been denied by mathematicians and geometricians owing to the fact that they have thought of it as a mathematical problem rather than a geometrical one and a metaphysical one. It is utterly impossible for one to accomplish the work in a physical way; it must be done metaphysically and geometrically, not mathematically. When approached in this manner the problem is easy of solution.

It is stated by occultists that the number 12 squares the circle and it is necessary to take into consideration the process before we can understand this; when correctly understood we know it perfectly true.

What is meant by Squaring the Circle? The Circle is the symbol of unity; it is that which has neither beginning nor end, therefore, is the one principle. It is also, in a certain sense the trinity, namely, that the triangle is included within the circle. In some problems we use the circle as symbolizin the trinity, that is two in one. The quarternary of the circle is then this principle expressed in its fourfold manifestation. The Swastika gives us the key to the square process. The Circle represents the undifferentiated principle on whatever plane it may be and in some cases also the electrical and magnetic principles constituting the triangular form.

When the process of emanation begins we see the Circle acting in four different directions, namely through the positive and negative electricity and magnetism. Thus there flow forth the two principles in their twofold differentiation —the twofold forces. As these two principles spring forth

SQUARING THE CIRCLE

into being we have the four lower notes of each octave going forth as the four emanations. On the physical plane we have Earth, Water, Fire and Air proceeding from the trinity above, or electricity and magnetism, but as fire is positive electricity, and water negative, and as earth is positive magnetism and air negative, we may, therefore, include the two principles above, electricity and magnetism, with these four. That is to say, the Swastika represents four arms proceeding from a central point and in that central point the two cross, therefore, we have in that point the emergence, the electrical and magnetic, hence it is the one principle differentiating itself that way by mutual separation, so as to give expression to these four principles. Thus it is the Squaring of the Circle, that is the fourfold manifestation of unity, the same as in the desire octave, the unit expressing itself through the fourfold manifestation; likewise, on the mental octave, the Buddhic and the Nirvanic. These five octaves admit of the fourfold differentiation of the one principle, unity; in other words the quarternary of the circle. Thus we may say, this differentiation presents itself on all the planes of Nature. Further, we have the Spirit itself manifesting itself in the four lower principles. We may say this is one aspect of the quarternary of the circle. The Spirit, which is the circle, manifests itself through Atma, Buddhi, Manas, a Triad, or the True. This matter is the fourfold differentiation of spirit, but the Squaring of the Circle means for the one principle to differentiate so as to form the fourfold manifestation, which we see in the quarternary on each plane. This, as was said before, is the Squaring, in one sense, of the Trinity.

Now we come to the mathematical Squaring of the Circle, that is the number 12. Twelve is four times three; in other words, it is three squared; that is three in four opposite directions, but three is the symbol of trinity; it represents the law of opposites swallowed up in the law of balance; the electric and magnetic principles bent together, fastened, united by the neutral principle, a perfect union, two in one; this is the signification of trinity taken mathematically. Trinity, therefore, represents the undifferentiated principle of positive and negative, or more properly, electric and magnetic principles connected, but undifferentiated. Thus Trinity stands alone, occupying the three higher notes of the octave no matter what they may be. If it be the physical trinity then it represents the ether, electricity and magnetism. When squared it represents, Earth, Water, Fire and Air, and on the other planes it is the same way, the four lower namely, the odoriferous, gustiferous, luminiferous and tangiferous ethers, and the manifestation or expression of the higher ether, which is the trinity. Thus we have the fourfold manifestation or trinity expressing itself in four different directions, therefore, the trinity taken four times, therefore, four times three or twelve. Likewise, the fourth of twelve is three. That is to say the quarternary or manifestation may be reversed and all the manifested resolved into the trinity; in other words, earth, water, fire and air and all the physical world may be returned back into electricity and magnetism, together with the undifferentiated ether. Likewise on all the other planes of nature, creation has been the expression of Squaring the Circle. It has been the manifestation of the trinity in its fourfold division. It is manifested in this way or as the circle squared. The Squaring of the Circle has been the work of every one who has accomplished anything of a creative character. It is, in other words, the descent of Spirit into matter that is represented by the Squaring of the Circle. Every emanation has been the Squaring of the Circle. One who has learned the art knows how to express trinity in the fourfold way and one who knows how to express trinity in this way knows the art of creation; he has mastered the mysteries of alchemy and magic and it is this problem that must be solved in accomplishing those things, namely, the descent of the higher trinity into the lower world by reason of the positive and negative separation and by reason of the electric and magnetic principles. When one has learned to do that he has mastered the Great Work.

So much for the Squaring of the Circle. But there is another side to the problem, namely, the Circling of the Square,—quite as important as Squaring the Circle. Now, inasmuch as the circle has expressed itself, manifested itself by its outflowing or outbreathing, the Circling of the Square

SQUARING THE CIRCLE

is to inbreathe, indraw the manifested principle, so that they return to the state from whence they came. In other words, Earth, Water, Fire and Air cease to be and are drawn back into the trinity of ether, electricity and magnetism—flowing in toward the center; in other words, Pralaya. Manvantara is the flowing out or unfolding from the center; Pralaya is the flowing in or infolding toward the center. This is what is meant by the Circling of the Square—the return to unity. It has a number of meanings, one of which is to bring the manifested universe into absolute harmony with the center from whence it proceeded and have it learn by its experiences how to find the center within. When one has learned this lesson, has mastered this problem, he knows how to overcome the obstacles of matter and make them a manifestation of spirit.

The Circling of the Square is emblematic of the close to which the world is moving; the state of life where the external or manifestation will be the perfect expression of the center. These outer expressions will no longer stand alone, but will reveal the inner being. The resistance, the immobility of the physical world will be brought under the influence of the electrical and magnetic forces. Thus we will enter upon a new era. But this is not all, because we found in studying the Squaring of the Circle, that the four lower octaves were but the squaring of the Spiritual or Nirvanic octave, therefore, when the square is circled these four will be swallowed up in the first, or fifth, as you prefer to call it, namely, the Nirvanic or spiritual, when the four lower octaves will perfectly express the spiritual. The eternal war between Spirit and Matter will thus be harmonized or compromised by the surrender of matter to spirit, in the sense that it is now governed by spirit. Spirit will be King—Ruler. All response in rebellion of matter will be at an end. Thus we will have the material square drawn back into the spiritual circle. Multiplicity will have been swallowed up in unity without losing the multiplicity; that is to say, unity will be multiplied, expressed and yet not lose itself, showing unity.

This is the realization of Nirvana for when the Square is circled the world will have returned to Nirvana. When any

OCCULT GEOMETRY

man circles the square in his own life, he has reached Nirvana, has overcome the three worlds and even the realm of soul and has entered the realm of the spirit. The domain of Nirvana is, therefore, the Circling of the Square in either the individual or the world.

There is another sense in which the square is circled; if one will not return to the center, but insists upon living in the outer world, sooner or later he will return to the center anyhow; that is, the manifested existence will be dissolved; thus the AMEN is reached. You may Circle the Square as an entity, or the entity may be destroyed and the square will be circled. Whether you will have it done as an entity or not, the entity will simply be obliterated and then the square will be circled. Again, any part of the universe that cannot be drawn into the circle, will be obliterated.

We see, thus the purpose of evolution, namely, the production of a type which manifests the perfection of the center, the expression of the center in the circumference without losing any of the fundamental nature of the center. This is the ultimate end of evolution. If you will not do this, or if the world will not do this, it must be reduced to chaos and worked out again. Thus the Kosmos must be thrown into chaos time and again until it can express the nature of the center in the circumference. When that is done the end of evolution will have been realized.

Thus the Circling of the Square is the returning of the manifested into that from which manifestation was produced. The drawing of the circumference into the center, while the Squaring of the Circle is the expression of the center in the circumference, and this is nothing more nor less than the Sankhya Philosophy of the Great Breath.

The Circling of the Square is the inbreathing, the Pralaya, and the Squaring of the Circle the outbreathing or Manvantara, but it is not a physical or mathematical, but the geometrical expression of a great metaphysical problem, or creation and destruction.

Squaring the Circle is the end of Brahman, while Circling the Square is the end of Shiva. In the two activities, in their perfect balance, we see preservative work, or Vishnu.

RALEIGH BOOKS AND LESSONS

Complete list of the Hermetic works by Dr. A. S. Raleigh, published in book form and which will be sent postpaid at prices listed:

The Central Spiritual Sun and The Virgin of the World	$ 1.00
The Lakshmi Avatar, Lakshmi and the Gopis	1.00
The Law of Karma	1.00
The Two Paths or the Parting of the Ways	1.00
Woman and Super-Woman	2.00
Shepherd of Men	2.50
Stanzas of Dzjn (Theogenesis)	5.00
Philosophia Hermetica	10.00
Scientifica Hermetica	10.00
Hermetic Art	10.00
Philosophy of Alchemy	10.00
Science of Alchemy	10.00
Speculative Art of Alchemy	10.00
Hermetic Science of Motion and Number	10.00
Hermetic Fundamentals Revealed	10.00
Hermetic Consciousness Unveiled	10.00
Magic	10.00
Occult Geometry	10.00
Phrenogarten Course (explains the brain)	10.00
Metaphysical Healing, Volume I	7.50
Metaphysical Healing, Volume II	7.50
Interpretation to Rudyard Kipling's Story, Brushwood Boy and the Map	7.50
Interpretation to Rudyard Kipling's Story, They	7.50

Manuscript Lessons, nicely typed and bound.

The Secret Sermon on the Mount or the Way of Rebirth	10.00
Interpretation to Henry Van Dyke's Story, The Other Wise Man	5.00

We also make a specialty of rare, out-of-print books along the line of Occultism, Mysticism, the Kaballa, the Tarot, Magic, Alchemy, Symbolism, Mythology, Rosicrucianism, Hermeticism and kindred subjects. A circular showing titles and prices of our list of rare, out-of-print books will be sent free of cost upon request.

HERMETIC PUBLISHING COMPANY

3006 Lake Park Ave.   Chicago, Ill., U. S. A.

CPSIA information can be obtained at www.ICGtesting.com
Printed in the USA
BVOW02s1002140814

362905BV00029B/974/P